"In the less-than-an-hour it takes to read this powerful treatise you will be motivated and equipped to lead transformational change in your school setting. If thorny issues such as diversity, low achievement, and motivation are concerns for your setting, you will find here concrete, doable ideas for action."

David J. Barker
Chair, Illinois Advisory Council on Bilingual Education
Retired Principal, Maine East High School, IL

"Mental Karate has helped our students see things in themselves they might have never seen."

Laurel Lemley
Teacher, Leon HS, FL

"Mawi is able in simple and elegant language to convey profound truth with brevity and sincerity."

Richard Marius
Senior Lecturer, Harvard University

P9-CBW-710

"I have confidence – something that I never really had before this year. I stopped cutting myself. I was always afraid that one day I would come home and be so upset I would slit my wrists. And all of these things have caused me to smile so much more."

Abbie

13-year-old, VT

"Once in a while you hear someone who can change your thoughts, attitude, and your life. Mawi Asgedom is one such person."

Aaron Redd & Kerry McQuade

two teenagers writing in local paper

"Asgedom has taken the disparate things life has given him up to now, bound them together to make them whole, and transformed them into something solid for the nourishment and use of others."

Harvard Magazine

"Mawi Asgedom is a hero to me and my students."

Pat Martin

Superintendent, St. Paul Public Schools

"Since then I have made A's and B's and I haven't got into any trouble with the police. I quite smoking and drinking and stopped hanging out with the people that I used to, and I feel like a whole new person. I want to thank you so much for inspiring me to do the right thing."

Krista

High School Freshmen, Winter Haven, FL

"Mental Karate has been the best thing in my life."

Angelo Soto

Barrington Prairie Middle School, IL

"Mental Karate has exceeded our expectations."

Art Fessler

Principal, Barrington Prairie MS, IL

"Our students attended your speech at Warner Bros studios. Since seeing and meeting you, they are setting their own goals and striving to reach them."

Hallie Fleischman

School Counselor, John Muir Middle School

"Mawi's practical advice will motivate teens to greater levels of success."

Booklist

"Mawi's books provide a powerful way for us to help thousands of teens across the country develop skills for success."

Allison Burns-Ferro

Director of Corporate Relations, Time Warner

"Your materials are working here at Rolling Meadows High School."

Liz Brandt

English Teacher, Rolling Meadows, IL

"Amazing!"

Oprah Winfrey

Beyond Character Education

Beyond
Character
Education
The
Case
for
Character
Action

Mawi Asgedom

Copyright © 2009 by Mawi Asgedom. All Rights Reserved.

Published by Mawi, Inc   www.mawispeaks.com

Publisher's Cataloging-in-Publication

Asgedom, Mawi.
Beyond Character Education: The Case for Character Action/author
Mawi Asgedom. 1st ed.

ISBN: 0-9743901-2-7

1. Asgedom, Mawi   2. Character Education

Printed in the United States of America

Interior and exterior design by Dan Elliott   ligaturestudio.com

Quantity discounts are available on bulk purchases. For more
information, please email info@mawispeaks.com

Dedicated to my beautiful wife Erin.

Books by Mawi

Of Beetles and Angels

The Code

Win the Inner Battle

Mimic the Devil

The Third Harmony

Beyond Character Education

Audio

Nothing Is Impossible
(4 Inspiring speeches on CD)

Bulk Discounts of the above titles are available by emailing info@MawiSpeaks.com

Contents

Introduction

"I know of no more encouraging fact than the unquestionable ability of man to elevate his life by conscious endeavor."

Henry David Thoreau
1817—1862

Today, at thousands of middle and high schools, you will find walls adorned with words such as responsibility, respect, and discipline. You will find passionate, dedicated educators planning months ahead of time to invite inspirational speakers who can help bring these words to life. You will find principals reviewing mission statements with their staff, parents, and students.

More ambitious schools will require service learning hours or Mix-It-Up days where students eat lunch with randomly assigned classmates. Other schools might require their students to read leadership guides such as *The 7 Habits of Highly Effective Teenagers.*

This focus on character is laudable. After all, students with "good" character should achieve higher; good character matters as much if not more than one's academic success; and many homes and community institutions no longer instill character as they once did.

There's just one problem: **Character education, in its current and dominant form at schools, is obsolete.**

Not that character education is useless. Typewriters are obsolete but we can still use them to write books. In the same way, we can do many positive things with character education. Unfortunately, giving students the internal skills they need today is not one of them.

Consider the world our young people live in. Corporations spend tens of billions, hiring graduates from top business schools with one clear goal: To shape what our youth eat, drink, watch, wear, hear, and consume. That's what our thirteen year olds are up against: a Harvard MBA with a billion dollar budget and an army of number crunchers. Armed with a speech and a poster, will our youth prevail?

In the old days, we could protect our young people, put guard rails around them, make sure they didn't see any obscene images, and keep them away from strangers. We could limit their interactions with unsavory peers or even choose which peers they interacted with. Now there are cell phones, MySpace, Twitter, Facebook – before this book is printed there will no doubt be new ways for youth to connect to virtually anyone at anytime.

Shifts of equal magnitude have revolutionized the business world. Previous generations could start and finish a career at the same company. Today's young adults exit school into a marketplace characterized by mercurial careers and globalized companies that shift both unskilled and skilled labor to the cheapest country. Given this new landscape, character principles like initiative can no longer remain posters on a wall or words in a speech; they must become tools our youth readily wield to create new opportunity for themselves and our world.

Today, more than ever before, our youth must proactively develop their own minds. For the abilities to exercise discipline, set goals, or persevere are no longer matters of character or achievement.

They are matters of survival.

Of course, our schools are already under tremendous pressure to meet rigid curriculum and achievement standards. High-stakes testing determines adequate yearly progress (AYP) and probationary status; in some states testing even determines whether students graduate or advance to the next grade.

Amidst this pressure, educators are understandably busy trying to meet standards in areas where they will be held accountable—core subject areas such as math and reading. So while many educators would agree that character matters, many more are simply overwhelmed by their existing workload.

Yet character can be an indispensable ally that catapults schools beyond their achievement goals. Consider the difference between a student who demonstrates discipline and a student who does not. Which student is more likely to consistently do their homework? Consider a student who demonstrates perseverance versus one who does not. Which student is more likely to soldier past challenging sections of an exam?

Character also affirms our basic humanity. After all, will students care about tests if schools do not first care about students—not as AYP scores but as human beings? Can we expect educators to exude passion if we turn educators into test-prep specialists?

My own story is a testament to the power of passionate, caring educators. I came to this country as a refugee at age seven. I spoke no English and literally came from living in a straw-thatched hut in Sudan. From first grade to senior year, my family lived on welfare, using food stamps to obtain food and living in government subsidized housing.

I had one equalizer in this country. One opportunity that trumped race and income: Education. I can write this book because my first grade ESL teacher met with my parents and convinced them to enroll me in supplementary summer school. I can write this book because my 4th grade librarian challenged me to read sixty books even though I had just graduated from ESL. I can write this book because my high school track coach paid for my running shoes all four years and bought me something I had never owned before: a pair of khaki pants.

Yes, I can write this book because I had a junior year English teacher who demanded that we use words like gossamer, duplicity, ephemeral, evanescent, and hackneyed in our papers. I can write this book because my guidance counselor encouraged me to apply to Harvard and even helped me move in when my parents couldn't.

I will never forget that **I would be nothing without my teachers and coaches and counselors and librarians.** Nor will I forget the importance of a winning mindset. Though I was relatively poor and an immigrant, I could still take initiative, show discipline, and persevere. In the same way, our youth can ascend to new heights by unlocking their own internal powers.

Over the last decade, I've studied how educators and youth can collaborate to create inspiring results. I've spoken at more than 1000 schools in almost forty states, often as a part of character education programs. By invitation, I have trained educators at The Harvard

School of Education, The Midwest Principals Center, and countless national conferences.

I've also had the honor of learning from some of the most skilled educators on the planet. One of my closest school partners, Vincent Massey School, just won the highest quality award offered by the country of Canada—the only school to do so. Another one of my school partners went from being the only middle school on the twelve most violent schools in New York list, to being a school openly lauded in the *New York Times* by the head of the NY schools.[1]

In the coming pages you will find the sum of my personal and professional knowledge on character development. You are busy so I've kept this book to just two chapters. In the first chapter I demonstrate that character education, in its dominant form at schools, is obsolete. In the second chapter, I offer practical solutions that will help any educator go beyond traditional notions of character education to unlock new levels of achievement.

---

[1] The school is J.H.S. 22 in the South Bronx, led by Principal Shimon Waronker.

Not that I have all the answers—I don't. I do know, however, that we can create a far richer character development paradigm that helps educators exceed performance standards and prepares students to succeed in today's globalized world.

Chapter One
Character Education is Obsolete

"Ideas without action are worthless."

Helen Keller
1880–1968

Before I lay out my basic argument, let's adopt a common definition. Character education is a loose term that defines internal development in two intertwined areas: moral development and effectiveness. Moral development consists of qualities such as citizenship, loyalty, and honesty. Effectiveness consists of habits such as initiative and discipline.

In simpler terms, character education is education about the internal resources that anyone can harness to achieve and live a "good, productive" life. At most schools, character education consists of some mix of inspirational speakers, inspiring posters, books on effectiveness, anti-bullying workshops, food drives, mission statements, leadership conferences for select students, homeroom advisories, and Citizenship Days.

I've personally worked with hundreds of wonderful educators who have spearheaded character education programs. This book does not detract from the impact these tremendous educators have had. Speeches *can* inspire students. Leadership books *can* teach effectiveness. Mission statements *can* help set the right tone.

This book simply aims to go beyond the traditional character education paradigm to a new, more impactful model. Before I present this new model, allow me to support the following assertion: **The current character education model has severe limitations that render it obsolete.**

Action

The most troubling aspect of the current character education paradigm is that it requires so little action. Students who learn about courage or respect today are rarely pushed in a systematic, organized manner to implement their new learning the following week or even the next day. Hence, short-term initiatives such as Citizenship Days usually do not translate into consistent, improved action by students.

Consider a guest speaker that speaks on the topic of courage. Would a school challenge every student to take five acts of courage in the month immediately following the speech? Would a school compile and measure those actions? For most of our schools, the answer is no.

We would never teach core subjects like Math and Reading without consistency, demonstration, independent practice, and assessment. If character development really mattered as much as people say it does, would we not require the same?

Many schools require students to read books on leadership or success. But how many schools actually require students to apply what they read in a clear, measurable way? How many schools measure student application?

Think of the most basic character principle: Initiative. This simple concept—that one is empowered to take action—is the foundational principle of almost every leadership and character education manual. Yet how many schools measure the acts of initiative they have helped students take? We measure math scores. We measure reading scores. **If character development was important, wouldn't we try to put metrics around student action?**

The gap between theory and action, by the way, is not a middle school or high school issue. I earned a Masters degree from Northwestern University's Kellogg School of Management and I can assure you, the Deans always spoke of the importance of character and leadership. The school provided countless speakers on courage, honesty and other principles. But rarely, if ever, did the school assess us to see what actions we had taken as a result of all these wonderful speeches. We took surveys at the beginning and end of our tenure, but did little in between to consistently measure or track our internal progress. You will find the same at Harvard and most other universities. At all levels, our educational institutions have a culture of speaking, posting, and reading. But the link to action is often missing.

My advice to schools may seem strange since I earn much of my living as a speaker: Do not hire any character education speakers if you are not going to challenge your students to take clear, measurable actions as a result of the speech. Do not buy any books like my book *The Code: The 5 Secrets of Teen Success* if you are not going to immediately challenge students to take actions connected to the principles in the book. Save your money. Take the kids on a field trip or something else.

Because the power of character can only be harnessed one way: Action.

Lifestyles

Middle and high school educators already know that most character education programs lose effectiveness as students get older. Character Counts and DARE sometimes gain acceptance among elementary age students but not so much from teenagers. A part of it, certainly, is that teenagers are naturally much more skeptical and much less malleable than eight year olds.

But something much larger than teen skepticism is at work: Lifestyles.

Lifestyles are universal systems of living and acting. They connote a certain group of friends; clothing, lingo, and an intangible vibe that includes how a student stands and looks you in the eye. Of course, lifestyles also directly influence many things educators care about such as academic drive and attendance.

You already know many of the teen lifestyle options: Hip-Hop, Goth, athletics, and youth group. For example, a common caricature of the Hip-Hop lifestyle might be baggy jeans, gold chains, irreverence for authority, a belief that one can be "discovered" or made rich at any time, toughness, intolerance for being "disrespected," and sexual promiscuity.

Regardless of how you define Hip-Hop or any other lifestyle, one thing is clear: Recent changes in technology have drastically increased the power of lifestyles. Ten years ago, students interested in Goth lifestyle could live it with their friends at school, by attending concerts, and hanging out after school.

Now, students can live that lifestyle 24/7. They can shop at thousands of online stores for the perfect gear. They can instant message, text message, Twitter, Faceboook, Myspace, and YouTube their friends and lifestyle every waking moment. They can throw parties with a text message's notice.

Why does all this matter? **Schools are setting up character education programs but students are living lifestyles**. Character education has stayed static, but the world students live in has radically changed, becoming much more dynamic.

Even as the power of lifestyles has skyrocketed, the dominant lifestyle that schools offer has stagnated, becoming increasingly narrow and unpalatable for students. Budgets at schools have shifted; curricula have shifted, all towards one goal: raising student test scores.

Hence, students navigating the turbulence of adolescence face a double-whammy: The power and allure of external lifestyles has increased while the power and allure of school culture has decreased. While our schools are trying to raise test scores, our students are trying to LIVE.

If the influence of lifestyles sounds overwhelming, be heartened. In the next chapter on solutions, I will offer some clear, simple methods that schools are already using to create and co-opt positive lifestyle options while creating a school culture that appeals to students.

The main takeaway, though, is that programs are obsolete. Think culture. Think lifestyle. Because a lifestyle will demolish a program any day of the week.

Discipline

It is not possible to speak of character without speaking of discipline, the simple concept that small daily actions can generate unimagined, even shocking results. In fact, I challenge you to find a respected character or leadership training guide that does not have discipline as a cornerstone.

Unfortunately, the dominant messages in our society, particularly messages aimed at youth, are the opposite of discipline. You can have whatever you want, today, for very little work. Dreams can be accomplished just because you dreamed, not because you worked consistently. Success is always just a heartbeat away.

Advertisements flash this quick success message everywhere. Need a loan? Want to lose weight? Are you lonely? We have a quick, easy, costless solution for you today.

Of course, any thinking person, anyone who has actually accomplished anything, knows that success comes from taking small, consistent steps, day after day.

With discipline in mind, then, consider Figure 1. How many of our schools are in the quick-fix column that characterizes much of character education? How many of our schools also lament, **"We've had a character education program for years and nothing has really changed?"**

Figure 1

	Character Education	New Paradigm
Focus	Students hear or read about someone else's inspiring journey.	Students go on their own inspiring journey.
Scope	Compartmentalized into a few isolated events/initiatives.	Part of a school's DNA and culture.
Time Frame	Limited: A speech, a citizenship day, a courage month.	Year-long pursuit of continuous, positive action.
Methodology	Shifting: courage focus one year; compassion the next.	Consistent: clear structure with a **bias for action.**
Results	Unclear: Hard to identify specific actions taken by students.	Clear, specific actions both at individual and aggregate levels.

The time has come to ask ourselves: Can a one-hour inspirational speech substitute for a yearlong, week-by-week focus on inspired action? Will a poster or a Citizenship Day suffice to give our students the internal tools they need in the 21st century?

One school near my home teaches character by having teachers fill out a worksheet with students once a month for forty-five minutes. Will that forty-five minute worksheet show students how to unlock their internal powers?

We all know the reasons to choose the quick-fix, less rigorous methods. Quick-fix costs less time. Less money. Less effort.

And it promises a big reward. Sound familiar?

Negative Definition

If schools had to choose just one character quality they wanted youth to embody, many schools would choose respect. Academic success, talent, drive – do any of these things matter if one does not have a basic respect for fellow human beings?

To analyze how respect is often taught, let's look at its opposite: disrespect. Schools are generally proficient at defining disrespectful behavior. No swearing. No fighting. No cheating on exams. No talking back to teachers. No unexcused absences. No bullying.

Our schools are also good at classifying kids into two general buckets: the "good" kids and the "bad" kids. Good kids, of course, follow the above rules; bad kids don't.

Most schools, by necessity, also have an elaborate system for monitoring the bad or disrespectful kids. Deans, principals, assistant principals, security officers, teachers, and other staff patrol the hallways, call parents, and discipline students.

But let's forget the "bad" kids for a moment. Focus instead on the basic requirements to be considered one of the "good" or one of the "respectful" kids. What are they? Show up most days, avoid getting a referral or suspension, turn in your homework, and you are one of the "good" kids.

Let me repeat: You don't actually have to do anything distinctively good; just avoid the bad things and you will be on par.

The adult version of this is with neighbors. If a neighbor avoids throwing loud parties and keeps weeds out of their lawns, they are by many accounts a decent neighbor. Again, the metric is the absence of something bad not necessarily the presence of anything distinctively good such as mowing a neighbor's lawn, or caring for an elderly neighbor, or keeping an eye on a neighbor's kid.

Of course, we've all experienced how wonderful it is when someone *does* do something proactively respectful. When my family came to the U.S. from Sudan, we did not know how to walk to our elementary school. I will never forget a freckled, good-natured 3rd grader named Brian Willmer who walked us back and forth every day until we knew the way. Years later, when my family lived on welfare in low-income housing, we had a washing machine that broke frequently. We could not afford to fix it nor could we afford to purchase a new machine. Each time the machine broke, a local high school principal named Dr. Fantozzi came and fixed it. I still remember Dr. Fantozzi extended on the cement ground, perspiring while fidgeting with his flashlight.

What would our schools be like if we consistently challenged students to show proactive respect like that shown by Brian or Dr. Fantozzi? Instead of spending so much time and effort trying to keep the "bad' kids from doing "bad" things, what if we challenged all kids to proactively show respect for each other and their larger community. Instead of trying to prevent bullies, what if we told the rest of the student body: If you do not help stand up to bullies, *you* are a bully.

We know what the list of disrespectful behaviors looks like. **What would the list of twenty proactively respectful behaviors look like?** What if schools held students just as accountable for the good as the bad?

I once heard someone say that "We lose our youth not because we challenge them too much but because we do not challenge them enough." Let's stop defining respect in the negative, and instead challenge students to proactively develop the positive aspects of their character.

Training

Earlier, I pointed out that we provide educators with little formal training on character development. You might ask: Why would training be necessary?

If character education is hiring a speaker, hanging a poster on the wall, and reading a book with students, then training may not be necessary. In fact, I've worked with many rotating PTA Presidents who have done a wonderful job bringing in guest speakers.

But if character education means helping students understand and proactively harness their internal powers, then a little training might be in order. Why? Because the power within is often murkier and more complex than one might think.

For example, consider the concept of self-esteem. For decades in this country, there has been a self-esteem movement. Teachers and parents have carefully reminded students that each student is unique, beautiful, and wonderful. Students have been encouraged to watch the words they say to each other, for words can affect self-esteem.

It's hard to argue: Words are indeed powerful and every child is unique and beautiful. Guess what the research shows, though. Research conducted for decades by leading psychologists such as Martin Seligman shows that true, enduring self-esteem comes from acquiring skills and mastery, not just from words. Learn to play the piano. Your self-esteem will rise. Learn how to spell forty new words. Your confidence rises. **Turns out we should have had a "Skill Acquisition" as well as a "Self-Esteem" movement.**

Consider another example that shows the complexity of character development. This last decade, I have been asked many times to speak on the character principle of perseverance, not just by schools but by Fortune 500 companies. For the first five years, I challenged my audiences not to give up and told them numerous stories of individuals who persevered, including my own mother who led my family to a Sudanese refugee camp. The speeches were generally very well received.

Then, prompted by a school counselor, I did some research to see what science says about perseverance. Turns out that there's a lot more to perseverance than just saying the words, "Don't Give Up" or "Stay Strong."

Research shows that perseverance actually consists of three abilities:

1. The ability to view challenges as temporary rather than permanent
2. The ability to view challenges as limited in scope rather than pervasive
3. The ability to not beat oneself up inordinately[2]

What's more useful to a young person facing a challenge: telling them not to give up, or training them to understand and apply these three keys to persevere? Yet I guarantee you that over 90% of speakers and schools just repeat the "Don't Give Up" lines without actually teaching their audience HOW not to give up – I myself was one of those speakers for years.

How is always harder than just telling someone to do something. *How* to have self-esteem, *how* to persevere, *how* to accomplish a goal; these are much harder than just saying "Don't give up, or "Believe in yourself."

---

[2] You can learn more about the science of resilience and self-esteem by reading *The Optimistic Child* by Martin Seligman.

Think about it. What does it actually mean when we tell a young person that they have "tremendous power within?" It means nothing, right? It's a nice sounding platitude but that platitude alone will not show a young person how to unlock that power.

Complexity is the first reason for training – we need to give students and educators more depth in their understanding of the power within, in understanding words such as self-esteem and perseverance.

But there may be even larger reasons for training. Consider progression. In math, we know that a student should progress from addition to subtraction to multiplication to division, then fractions and decimals and so forth. In writing, we know they should learn the alphabet, basic print, then cursive, basic grammar and spelling, advanced reading and writing, and so forth. But what is the progression for students when it comes to inner development? Should they learn goal-setting first, then initiative, then courage?

Because there's no definitive paradigm that conclusively defines inner development, schools often seesaw between different approaches. *Let's learn about courage today. Two months from now, let's do goal setting. Let's bring in a speaker on diversity.* All these efforts are indeed commendable, but they lack a precise, logical methodology that gives students a clear, comprehensive structure for understanding their internal powers and how those internal powers can help them in their daily lives. Without an end goal, without a logical progression to guide them, students progress either randomly, or not at all.

Adding to the confusion, inner development is hard to measure. I can tell whether you answered a math problem correctly or whether your English paper was written well. But how do I measure four units of initiative or eight units of perseverance? What does a 93% for character mean? Because character can be hard to measure, many schools choose not to measure it at all.

I could go on and on about why we need training. For example, there may be no greater wrong we've inflicted on our young people than the faulty definition of talent we've taught them. Schools in general define talent as the ability to take tests, memorize, and spit back information. Do that and you get A's.

In contrast, the business world defines talent in a MUCH broader way. A salesperson needs the ability to establish rapport and persevere in the face of rejection; an investigative reporter needs a proclivity for skepticism; a great manager needs an ability to bring out each employee's best.[3]

The "real world" expands the talents necessary for success. Yet at many schools, we limit students by making them believe they have no future if they do not have the narrow talents associated with being in the top 5% or scoring well on the SAT.

---

[3] You can learn more about how businesses define talent by reading the book, *Now Discover Your Strengths* by Marcus Buckingham.

Complexity. Progression. Measurement. Talents. What is the point of all this? Character development, while simple on the face, requires knowledge and depth to understand and teach.

So if we're serious about character education, we need to establish new formal training for educators. Otherwise, expect more speakers and posters that offer encouragement but don't actually show students HOW to harness the power within.

Summary

Whether you're convinced or not, I hope that you learned at least one thing from this chapter. Here again are the key reasons that I believe the current model of character education is obsolete:

1. We do not challenge students to take action.
2. We offer character education programs that cannot compete with lifestyles.
3. We offer character education programs that are largely one-time, quick-fix, and easy, rather than consistent and demanding.
4. We define respect more by an absence of negative than a presence of positive.
5. We fail to properly train educators on how to teach character development.

In the next section, please find some solutions and a portrait of what a new paradigm might look like.

Chapter Two
Character
Action

"You become just by performing just actions,
temperate by performing temperate actions,
brave by performing brave actions."

Aristotle
384–322 BC

Change the Name

We don't speak of iceboxes because iceboxes are obsolete. We don't speak of typewriters because typewriters are obsolete. In the same way, let us speak no more of character education. Instead, let us speak of character action.

To see why nomenclature matters, compare the difference between these two questions at a planning meeting:

"What should we do this year for character education?"

"What should we do this year for character action?"

The first question will lead you to focus on the message you want to communicate. The latter, on the actions you want students to take. It's the same difference between majoring in math, which is theoretical, and applied math, which one applies.

Same thing with guest speakers. **We should speak no longer of guest speakers, but instead, of action speakers.** Of course, schools must partner with speakers to change the paradigm from education to action. After all, students are unlikely to take action after a speech if they lack time to brainstorm what actions they might take.

No more leadership books, but leadership action books. Before purchasing any new character development books, schools should first plan out how those books will help students take new, more inspired action. Same thing with the many leadership conferences I've spoken at – change the name from leadership conference to leadership action conference. All the conferences in the world will not teach character and leadership if students go back home and keep doing what they were doing prior to the conference.

In the end, it's simple: Either words like initiative and respect have power or they don't. If they don't have power, let's stop talking about character and use that class time and wall space for other purposes.

If they do, let's unlock that power through action.
Character Action.

Measure Action

Character, because it is internal, is often very hard to measure. But measure it we must, for we cannot improve what we cannot measure.

Let me share a method I've helped my school partners use to stimulate and measure character. It's simple: Just require a set number of actions connected to any character principle. For example, schools can measure initiative simply by asking each staff member and student to take three specific acts of initiative in a given month.

At one school I worked with, a student wrote to a mother who was in jail. Another student started studying piano again. A teacher read three times a week to his five-year-old son. Another teacher applied to a writing program and was accepted. Students and staff tracked all their actions in journals and by the end of the month, we had hundreds of concrete acts of initiative. All of this happened because instead of learning about initiative, we sought to unlock initiative's power through action.

Of course, you can find many reasons why this method of measurement is flawed: Some of the students and teachers might have lied about their actions; some of the actions required more initiative than others, etc. Do not let the flaws stop you.

Instead, expect Character Action to be harder than Character Education. Why? Because taking action is much harder than hanging a poster on the wall or having students sit for a presentation. Application is always harder, in all aspects of life. Is it not easier to give a lecture on the quadratic formula than to have all the students apply the quadratic formula on their own?

Look at it this way: When your school board asks you what happened with all that character development money, do you want to list the speakers you invited and the books students read? Or do you want to list the concrete actions taken by students and staff at your school?

Increase the Scope

Consider Figure 1 from earlier.

Figure 1

	Character Education	Character Action
Focus	Students hear or read about someone else's inspiring journey.	Students go on their own inspiring journey.
Scope	Compartmentalized into a few isolated events/initiatives.	Part of a school's DNA and culture.
Time Frame	Limited: A speech, a citizenship day, a courage month.	Year-long pursuit of continuous, positive action.
Methodology	Shifting: courage focus one year; compassion the next.	Consistent: clear structure with a **bias for action.**
Results	Unclear: Hard to identify specific actions taken by students.	Clear, specific actions both at individual and aggregate levels.

The Character Education column requires less effort, less planning, less action. It lets students off the hook by focusing students on someone else's journey.

By moving to the rigorous, character action column, we can challenge students to create their own inspiring journeys. We can challenge students to create specific, measurable results. We can offer a clear, logical methodology that makes sense to students and staff alike.

Of course, this is easier said than done. Many educators are already overwhelmed by their existing curricula. Every school has a different schedule, staff openness to new ideas, political climate and funding reality. And educators have varying levels of interest in character development in the same way that educators have varying levels of interest in math or English.

Of course, schools DO make room in the curriculum and DO provide funding if something is deemed important enough. So the question isn't, "Is Character Action challenging," but rather "How much of a priority is Character Action?" Because if schools want to do it right, there's no way around it: Schools have to commit time and resources.

Once schools commit, the path forward is not necessarily clear. Character Action is still in its infancy—nowhere near as developed as Character Education.

As you review your options, I can offer you three resources. First of all, you can use Figure 1 as a litmus test for Character Action. For example, anything that requires limited action will generate limited results. **Anything that is compartmentalized into a few, isolated initiatives will not become part of a school's DNA and culture**.

The second resource is a hub where we can all share Character Action best practices with each other. Go to CharacterAction.com and you will find articles, curriculum ideas, and training opportunities such as an annual summer conference. You can also see examples of Character Action models and share your own.

As an example, let me share something I learned from a wonderful English teacher named Sara Kahn. Sara taught Nelson Mandela's memoir, *Long Walk to Freedom*, to her 8th graders. As her students read about Mandela's life, she asked them to pinpoint key times when Mandela harnessed the power of initiative. After the students discussed these times, Sara challenged each student to take initiative and to journal about it.

Rather than seeing Mandela as some inaccessible, mythical figure, students made the connection to their own lives and saw that they too could harness the principles that led to his greatness. All this, while meeting state reading and writing standards.

I've met many wonderful, passionate educators like Sara who have come up with new ways to connect character to action. Since we are all busy, there's no point in each of us reinventing the wheel. Instead, let's come together to share ideas and grow together at CharacterAction.com.[4]

The third resource is Mental Karate, a Character Action journey I've created with the help of educators in the U.S. and Canada. Mental Karate is a tool that educators

---

[4] It is virtually impossible to acquire decent domain names these days. What does it tell you that in 2008, CharacterAction.com, .net, and .org were still available despite the countless character websites out there?

can use to stimulate and measure action. Examples of actions include: A student who feared public speaking demonstrated courage by joining the debate team; a student with severe physical challenges demonstrated discipline by climbing one flight of stairs each day for six weeks; a sophomore with a D in algebra demonstrated initiative by staying after-school for tutoring. The key is that students take action connected to proven principles such as initiative. You can see more examples and learn more at MentalKarate.com

Regardless of how you do it, Character Action requires a proactive commitment. It requires you to look at your many competing priorities and conclude that yes, rigorous character development is worth the investment.

Be Specific

Lifestyles, as we discussed earlier, are all-encompassing cultures that students can choose to embrace. Your school, of course, has its own culture, its own mini-lifestyle that is as invisible and real as the air you breathe.

How one is greeted by the secretary. The security system. Cleanliness. The number of students wandering the halls during class. Eye contact from students. The looks on students' faces.

Two minutes – that's all it takes to know what kind of school a school is. In those two minutes, both students and staff intuitively grasp whether character is just another program or a vibrant, appealing lifestyle.

Whole books have been written about school culture, so I will spare you a treatise. I will, however share a few observations that may help you create a school culture that can offer the excitement and meaning offered by other lifestyles.

The first is the importance of specifics.

Let me start with an example. One of the things many schools talk about is how they want to create a culture of college-readiness. Principals nationwide have given speeches about being college ready and hung collegiate banners across their walls.

All this talk and signage can help set a positive tone. But cultures cannot hang on generalities alone – they need specifics. For example, what if a middle school that touted college-readiness challenged each 8th grader to live out the culture of college readiness by doing the following:

- Writing at least one 10-page paper.
- Learning how to calculate a GPA.
- Using primary sources to create an original argument.
- Filling out the common application at commonapp.org so students know what to expect in four years.
- Interviewing three people who went to college and writing a paper about it.
- Attending at least one collegiate sporting event.
- Going to at least one new setting/camp where they will need to make new friends.

What is more likely to result in a college-ready culture: just the words and posters; or the words plus clear specific actions that all students regularly take? Think back to a lifestyle like Hip-Hop – it has meaning because there are certain specific artists and styles of dressing that give Hip-Hop depth. In the same way, your school culture must have depth through specifics.

Let me give you another example. It is vogue these days to speak of having high expectations for all students. Yet, if one pushes folks to define what "high expectations" mean, one often uncovers more platitudes such as, "all our students can achieve," or "we believe in all students." Here's the best definition of high expectations I have encountered in my ten years working with schools. It comes from a school that went from being one of Texas's worst schools to one of their best. Students do their homework. That's it. Students who do not turn in assignments are required to go to ZAP (Zeros Aren't Permitted) sessions after school to make up assignments. Teachers even pull students from lunch to complete homework. Simple right, but how much better is this clear policy than the words "high expectations?"[5]

---

[5] The name of the school is Southmore Intermediate in Pasadena, Texas.

Culture requires structure. We often avoid structure because it is much harder than hanging a poster on the wall. But without structure, we risk devolving into a string of platitudes and quotes that have no chance of competing with external lifestyles.

So ask yourself: What specific habits and rituals can you put in place that will help your school create a compelling lifestyle?

Your Trump

While creating specific rituals and habits will help, that will not be enough. Remember what you are facing when it comes to the lifestyle war: billion-dollar budgets, indigenous youth movements, the innate suspicion many teens have of authority, school, and the world itself.

Despite these challenges, you have a trump card, a bona fide ace in the hole. Research study after research study has confirmed this trump card; in fact, whole school systems have been reconfigured to support it.

What is it? Your ability to connect with your students. Your ability to let them know that you believe in them, care for them, and view them as unique. In one word: relationships.

Given my own personal story, I've taken a keen interest in how those from humble beginnings accomplish the American Dream. Hard work and discipline are always a part of it. But what I've found is that nobody, including myself, can pull themselves up simply through their own effort.

Why? For two reasons. First, knowing that someone cares about you and expects something good of you is a powerful positive magnet that keeps you doing the right things in the face of temptations. The second, more subtle reason is that education is much more than just formulas and words. Education is understanding social systems, how things "work," what the landscape of life and success looks like. Students can best receive this socialization through positive relationships at home, but if not at home, at school.

Five years ago I was speaking at a correctional facility for teens. After my presentation, one of the students raised his hand and said something I'll never forget:

"I know you lived in a refugee camp, and had to immigrate to the States. But I still think our story is tougher for one reason: You had parents and teachers who supported and encouraged you. Few of us in this jail did. I'd rather be a refugee with guidance and love than a native born citizen of this country without love."

After reflecting on the guidance my parents, siblings, and community gave me, I had to agree with the student: **The greatest poverty is indeed a poverty of relationships.**

Still, as I pointed out in the last section, a general statement like "relationships are important" is not particularly helpful. Instead, we should ask the question, "How can schools set up specific structures that build positive relationships?"

Consider the case of Steve Hamlin, a middle school principal who harnessed the power of relationships to drive student achievement. Steve's school had sixty Hispanic students that came from predominantly low-income backgrounds and had lower attendance and grades than their counterparts.

Steve selected one teacher who had demonstrated an ability to connect with students and gave that teacher training on how to talk with students in a one-on-one setting. Steve gave that teacher time off during the school's three lunch periods. Each period, the teacher had lunch with two Hispanic students, for a total of thirty students per week. Thus, the sixty Hispanic students each had lunch with the teacher every two weeks.

During those lunches, the teacher came to know and understand each student; he also helped them set and track goals. As a result of the consistent guidance, grades, test scores, and attendance skyrocketed for those sixty students — attendance alone rose from 75% to 95%.

Here's the point: Steve could have just given a speech asking his staff to develop relationships. Instead, he dedicated staff and time to create a structure that built positive relationships. The challenge for all schools is to go beyond words and create structures that build positive relationships.

This is also a larger challenge for our society.

I've seen many effective structures set up by schools and communities to create relationships. An English teacher named Dr. Langlas taught his students Tae-kwon-doe during first period; an Upword Bounds program at Sonoma State helped minority and low-income youth apply to college; a national corporate mentoring program I worked with helped over 1000 kids a year read better.

I personally saw these three organizations create wonderful results. But all three organizations had their budgets cut to make way for more important priorities, such as providing test-prep training.

While on one hand, we talk about the importance of relationships, with the other hand, we often destroy structures that create relationships. We as a country need to understand: One way or another we will provide a relationship for all our young people, particularly those who lack one at home. Either that relationship will be with an educator/mentor, or it will be with a correctional officer.

So the question schools need to ask is: What clear, specific structures can we set up to foster positive relationships?

It's a Lifestyle

Have you heard the old adage, "If you can't beat them, join them?" A great way to compete with lifestyles is not to fight them, but instead, to mimic them.

Consider the case of Clayton Muhammad, an educator in Aurora, IL. In 2002, Aurora saw a severe outbreak of gang violence, largely as the result of fifteen gang leaders.

Instead of just decrying the gangs, Clayton asked the following question: If the gangs could offer an exciting and alluring lifestyle, why not the schools? If the gangs could provide connection, identity, and purpose, why not the larger community? So Clayton recruited fifteen young men and started a brotherhood called Boys To Men (B2M).

How you walk matters, he taught the young men. **How you dress matters. How you hold your head matters. How you treat women matters. Everything matters.**

Clayton got B2M coverage in the local paper. He took them on college visits that showed them how exciting college life was. And Clayton published a magazine and on each cover, a student wore a stunning outfit, looking much more like a model for Sean Jean than the boring stereotype of a successful student. Consider three stanzas from the Boys 2 Men creed:

WE KNOW

Our education is our greatest equalizer.

Our discipline is the best gift that we can give ourselves.

Our service is what makes us great.

Our culture is defined by our actions.

Our brotherhood is unique and unified.

WE KNOW

Failure is not an option.

Stereotypes must be shattered.

Obstacles must be overcome.

Barriers must be broken.

WE KNOW

Being phenomenal is a lifestyle.

When you change your mind, you change your life.

When you know better, you do better.

All men are created equal.

Some just achieve more and look better.

Trust us…We Know!

Lifestyle. Clayton understood that students wanted a lifestyle complete with allure, power, excitement, and hope. Today, the B2M lifestyle – not program – is reaching hundreds of young men and women and expanding to other schools.

B2M is not alone. Consider the "options" hour at Vincent Massey School. Once a week students join with students from other classes to pursue areas of personal interest such as Hip-Hop dance, drama, guitar, jewelry making, photography, movie making, and environmental issues.

Consider an educator named Laurie Beauvais in Rhode Island. Each year at her school, she organizes a March Madness basketball tournament where students of all backgrounds and abilities organize into randomly assigned teams and have their own tournament.

Fun. Excitement. Teamwork. These are the words students use to describe something they do at school every year. These are the words we want students to use when describing life at all our schools.

So ask yourself: How can you co-opt the fun and excitement of alternative lifestyles and weave it into the fabric of your own school? Better still, ask your students.

Summary

I've presented the following six actions that schools can take to move beyond Character Education to Character Action:

1. Call it Character Action.
2. Measure Character Action.
3. Commit time, professional development and resources.
4. Create culture through specific structures.
5. Counter negative lifestyle options through structured relationships.
6. Create a fun, exciting, alluring lifestyle of your own.

I also offered two resources:

- CharacterAction.com – a website that offers best practices and professional development.

- MentalKarate.com – A comprehensive character action journey that in 2008 alone generated over 50,000 actions.

Conclusion

"Action has magic, grace and power in it."

Johann Wolfgang von Goethe
1749–1832

Beyond Character Ed

I was leading a Character Action training at a conference recently when an audience member stopped me and said, "You are making all this character action stuff sound like magic."

At first, I was taken back, and during an awkward moment, tried to figure out a way to defuse the critique; to distinguish what I was talking about as real, and completely separate from the sleight of hand associated with magic.

But then I thought of a 7th grader who had used his power of discipline to learn basic French on his own. I thought of a freshman who used her power of compassion to care for an ailing father. I thought of my own teenage years, when I used my power of initiative to apply to ten colleges, praying I'd get financial aid at one of them.

And it hit me how right the audience member was. For if there is no magic in our inner powers of love, initiative, discipline, courage, and contribution, where can magic be found in this world?

Imagine that our youth unlocked the magic of character by taking millions of actions each year. Imagine that we measured and celebrated those actions.

What would all those positive, inspired actions mean for our students? For our schools? For our world?

How about you? What would it mean for you to take and measure inspired action in your own life? What could you accomplish? What could you contribute?

Speeches can inspire and books can certainly point the way.

But only one thing can move us forward: Action.

Character Action.

Acknowledgements

Special thanks to the following people who provided invaluable assistance in the creation of this book: Carol Hunter, Erin Hatch, Kate Mazukelli, Mehret Asgedom, Joanne Rooney, Libby Burmaster, David Barker, Laurie Beauvais, Clayton Muhammad, Victor Kore, Bob Jarvis, Steve Hamlin, Davis Scott, Renee Lane, Mike Olander, and my wife Erin.

Big thanks to Dan Elliott for the cover and interior design.

Partner
with
Mawi

Mawi is available to provide Character
Action training at schools and conferences.

Bulk discounts of Mawi's books are also available.
Please direct inquiries to **info@MawiSpeaks.com**.

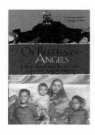

The body
copy of
this book
is set in
10/16 pt
Univers 55
on 60#
natural text

The cover is
printed on
12pt C1S cover

Designed
by
Ligature
Studio

ligaturestudio.com

Mawi Asgedom is widely recognized as one of North America's leading authorities on youth development. Mawi has written five books that are used in thousands of classrooms. Citing the impact of his books, The Illinois Association of Teachers of English named Mawi the 2006 Illinois Author of the Year. Mawi has spoken

About Mawi Asgedom

to over 500,000 students and trained educators at The Harvard School of Education, The Midwest Principals Center and countless national conferences.

As a child, Mawi fled civil war in Ethiopia and survived a Sudanese refugee camp for three years. After being resettled in The United States, Mawi overcame welfare, language barriers and personal tragedy to graduate from Harvard University.

Mawi has been featured by The Oprah Winfrey Show, *Chicago Tribune, Boston Globe, Harvard Magazine* and many other national media.

You can learn more about Mawi's work at **www.MentalKarate.com.**

3 MINUTES A DAY TO A 120 YEAR LIFESPAN

by Robert D. Willix, Jr., M.D.

Maximum Health

Meet Dr. Robert D. Willix, Jr.

Dr. Robert D. Willix, Jr., M.D.

To his friends, it seems that Dr. Robert D. Willix, Jr. has led several lives. The first was the life of a hell-raising young student athlete who didn't care much about his studies. That changed when a college professor saw his potential and steered him into graduate school in biology.

Soon that led to his second life as a medical student. . .and finally a hard-charging doctor who developed the only open-heart surgery program in the state of South Dakota.

But Dr. Willix decided to end his career as a famous and wealthy surgeon.

His latest life is the one that can change *your* life and help you live to be 90 or 100 years old — full of energy and in excellent health.

You see, Dr. Bob Willix is a *former* heart surgeon who decided to hang up his knife because he realized he wasn't helping people. The trauma of surgery left many patients ill and depressed. A few years after surgery, many had clogged arteries again and they were back under the knife.

Meanwhile, Dr. Willix found his own health was falling apart because of the same unhealthy habits that were killing his patients! He decided something was very wrong.

First, Dr. Willix changed his own life. He became healthy and happy.

In order to to do that, he chucked his lucrative career as a famous heart surgeon and embarked on a daring mid-life journey. For someone who was a doctor, it wasn't easy, but he came to believe the medical establishment is totally wrong about heart disease, stroke, cancer, and arthritis.

What's more, the medical system is so reluctant to change, it could cost you your life. This book will show you why, and what you can do about it.

But the good news is much more important: *Adopt Dr. Willix's way of looking at health, and there is no biological reason why you can't live to be over 100.*

Now in Florida he is helping thousands of people at his preventative medicine clinic — without drugs and surgery. And, as he explains it himself, he's saving many more lives than he ever did as a cardiac surgeon.

Contents

Chapter One

You Decide How Long You Will Live

Give me three minutes a day and I can add up to ten years to your life.

Give me an average of 16 minutes a day and I'll add as much as fifteen years to your life.

Give me one hour a day and I can add twenty years or more to your life.

Obviously, these figures are based on what an average person can achieve with my program. Your results may vary depending on your age and current state of health.

But the basic principle does _not_ vary: You can decide how healthy you will be and how long you will live. Even people who were old or in poor health have gotten well with my program.

**It really is possible to feel good all the time.** I mean more than just "not being sick." I mean actively _feeling good_. You can feel full of energy, with strong muscles, a

calm stomach, bones and joints free of stiff-
ness and pain, fresh and glowing skin, and
deep, easy breathing.

You can do it. It's all up to you. I know
because I was a stressed-out, 225-pound
surgeon. I smoked more than a pack a day
and followed a "seafood diet" (you see food
and you eat it). That was almost twenty years
ago. I was 34 and hadn't exercised since
college.

The Easiest Thing You Can Do For Your Health Is The Most Powerful

Let me just give you a peek at the powerful new medical discoveries.

A Harvard study shows that taking vitamin E long-term — more than two years —
can cut your risk of heart attack *almost in half*.
Yet only about four people out of a hundred
are taking enough vitamin E.

The Journal of the National Cancer Institute reported similar results for a study of
29,584 people in China, aged 40 to 69.

These people were poor. Their diet was
terrible. They had among the highest
esophageal and stomach cancer rates in the
world — over 100 times U.S. rates.

*Those who took a daily dose of beta
carotene, vitamin E and selenium suffered
9% fewer deaths than those who didn't*. These
three supplements are called *antioxidants*

(pronounced antee-oxy-dants). They are harmless vitamins and minerals found in our food. But we don't get them in large enough amounts to make us as well as we can be.

You're going to hear a lot about *antioxidants* in this book, because they are the most exciting medical discovery in fifty years.

Over the last few decades, evidence has been piling up higher than Pike's Peak that antioxidants are the key to preventing cancer, heart disease, arthritis and a host of other diseases.

There was a study of 3,318 Chinese who *already showed signs of cancer*. They were given a daily dose of 14 vitamins and 12 minerals for six years. There was an *8% decline in cancer deaths and a 38% reduction in stroke and heart disease*.

The Establishment
Almost Agrees

Two studies were presented in 1992 at the American Heart Association's 65th Scientific Sessions. The first study involved almost 90,000 women. Those who took vitamin E for more than two years **cut their risk of heart disease almost in half** compared to those who did not take vitamin E.

The second study involved 45,720 middle-aged and elderly men. Those who had taken *vitamin E for more than two years had a 26%*

lower risk of heart disease.

A recent study showed that people who regularly consume vitamin E supplements have *half the risk* of oral and pharyngeal cancer. That finding comes from researchers at the National Cancer Institute.

The NCI researchers also found that multivitamin tablets are not enough. You need big doses. Says one of the authors, "We speculate that the vitamin E dosage in multivitamins (usually 30 I.U.) was not sufficient for a protective effect."

It's fair to say the amount the goverment recommends — 10 I.U. — is pitifully inadequate to protect you against cancer.

If you want to be protected by this powerful antioxidant, you need to take vitamin E tablets containing anywhere from 100 to 400 I.U. (international units). You are not going to get what you need from One-A-Day. Let me add that no one has ever reported *any* toxic effect from taking large dosages of vitamin E.

We're living in the middle of a nutrition revolution. It turns out the easiest, most powerful way to improve your health is to take the vitamins and minerals called antioxidants.

All the diseases that have stumped the medical establishment—cancer, stroke, heart disease, aging — *have a single, underlying cause*. In a moment, I'm going to explain how it works. For now, I just want you to know it's quite easy to neutralize the killer.

Scientific research has clearly established the value of antioxidants. The pity is most of my colleagues in the medical profession don't know much about nutrition. But some of us are finally learning.

When I was in medical school, how much class time do you think I spent studying the effect on your body of the food you eat? I'll tell you: about four hours. And I spent *zero* hours studying the effect of exercise. Medical doctors just plain don't know this stuff. I had to learn it for myself.

Do One Thing Now —and Feel the Difference Within Two Weeks

Are you too busy to do *anything* to add years to your life? Or too broke? Or too skeptical to believe me?

If you fit any of these categories, at least try this: Take 200 micrograms (mcg.) of chromium picolinate. You can get it at any health food store or possibly your pharmacy.

You see, chromium enables you to convert sugar and fat into energy. If you will just try this harmless mineral for two weeks, you will have more energy. You may even start losing weight.

Lose weight while you sleep from taking a harmless pill. Not bad, huh?

About 90% of Americans don't get enough chromium. It's one of the reasons we're too fat. Many researchers now believe a lack of chromium is the culprit in 95% of all adult diabetes in our country. Sugar robs our bodies of this mineral and we need a lot of chromium just to balance out all the sugar we consume.

Chromium will help you stabilize your blood sugar level and get more energy out of the food you eat. It causes you to metabolize (burn your food) more efficiently. It actually burns up fat so you don't add it to the spare tire around your middle.

What's more, a researcher at the U.S. Department of Agriculture's Vitamin and Mineral Laboratory recently confirmed that chromium has no toxic effects. You can feel perfectly safe taking 200 mcg. per day.

Chances are, your doctor—who maybe had four hours of training in nutrition—will tell you supplements are a waste of time. Even after publishing the studies on vitamin E and beta carotene, the National Cancer Institute and the American Heart Association are *still* not recommending vitamins. They say "more study" is needed.

Chances are, you also heard all the recent media hoopla about a Finnish study showing beta carotene failed to protect against lung cancer. This burst of publicity completely misrepresented the findings and even contradicted what the authors of the study said themselves. There are more than 20 studies showing beta carotene is linked to *reduced* cancer rates. The National Cancer Institute has stated that every study on the carotenoids shows there is protection against lung cancer.

Citing this mountain of evidence, the authors of the Finnish study admit their findings "may well be due to chance." The subjects of their study were all pack-a-day smokers who had been smoking for 36 years, on average!

Meanwhile, the Finnish study also showed vitamin E reduced prostate cancer by 34%. For some reason, the media didn't trumpet that part. In sum, most news reports got the story totally wrong. I only hope and pray their misinformation doesn't cost any lives.

It's amazing.

In five or ten years, my fellow doctors are finally going to tell you to take vitamin A, vitamin E, beta carotene, selenium and other supplements. By that time hundreds of thousands of people will die who could have been saved.

If your doctor tells you not to take antioxidants, ask him if *he's* taking them. I bet he is. I know a lot of doctors who are taking antioxidants on the sly, because of the remarkable studies that are coming out.

Don't wait. Start taking these supplements at once. If you'd like monthly updates on the exciting new developments in this field, consider my newsletter *Healthy Longevity* (order form on page 121).

Meanwhile, turn to the next chapter and I'll tell you *why* these simple vitamins and minerals are so powerful at fighting cancer and heart disease.

Chapter Two

The Most Important Medical Discovery Of the Last Fifty Years

My aim is to put myself out of business — by making you healthy. The happiest day of my life is when a patient doesn't need me anymore.

The discovery I'm telling you about just might put a large part of the medical system out of business.

If people will just follow the suggestions in this chapter, the so-called health crisis in our country would largely disappear. Health spending would fall by one-third or more.

What scientists have found out is that *a single cause is responsible for aging as well as for cancer, heart disease, stroke, arthritis, and possibly allergies and a host of other ailments.*

These diseases are caused by much the same process that causes fuel to burn and oil to go rancid. The same process causes an apple to turn brown if you slice it open and expose it to the air.

The villain is oxygen — the same element that causes wood to burn and iron to rust. In a way, your body rusts from the inside out, causing dry, wrinkled skin, among other things. But aging skin is the least of our problems. When the process gets really out of control, it can cause cancer tumors and hardening of the arteries (athersclerosis).

Oxygen becomes harmful when it's combined into something called a *free radical. Free radicals are like ravenous molecular sharks*. These predators are so hungry they last only millionths of a second before they make a frenzied attack on a neighbor.

A free radical is not a living thing like viruses or bacteria. It's much smaller than that. It's a molecule. Viruses, bacteria, and all of the cells in your body are made up of molecules. Molecules are the building blocks.

The problem with a free radical is that it contains an oxygen atom that is missing an electron. A free radical can't rest until it replaces that missing electron, and generally the only place it can get an electron is by taking a bite out of another molecule. Your body is full of hundreds of billions of free radicals attacking your healthy cells.

The good news is that it's quite easy to control free radicals — now that we know what they are, and the harm they do!

Cancer, stroke and heart disease come in a bewildering variety of shapes. They seem to be caused by everything from smoking cigarettes to eating butter to pesticides. One type of cancer, like colon cancer, seems to have little to do with another type such as breast cancer. And both appear to have nothing in common with heart disease.

> Not until now, anyway! But now we know that all the diseases have the same underlying cause — free radicals.

Do you know why radiation can cause cancer? Because radiation creates free radicals.

Why does stress make us ill? It causes our bodies to form free radicals.

Why is smoking harmful? It creates free radicals. Ditto for air pollution and some of the pesticides in our environment. Even the chlorine in our water can form cancer-causing compounds that promote free radicals.

Why Your Doctor
Doesn't Want You to Know

The link between free radicals and the "aging diseases" is the most important discovery since doctors learned that some illnesses are caused by germs.

We've all learned to watch out for "germs." These viruses and bacteria cause diseases like colds, smallpox, typhoid, boils, TB, and so forth. Louis Pasteur pioneered the germ theory of disease over one hundred years ago. Most of the great successes of modern medicine have been due to this theory.

And those successes are *huge*. Smallpox and polio have been eliminated. There's very little TB and rheumatic fever anymore. Pneumonia is now treatable. We owe all this to modern medicine and the germ theory of disease.

But germs are no longer the big killers of our time. The big killers are cancer, stroke and heart disease. Our bodies are also wracked by allergies, arthritis, headaches, and chronic fatigue. *These diseases are not caused by germs.* The medical establishment doesn't know what causes them. *It doesn't have a clue as to what to do about them.*

Your doctors may talk a good line. They may throw a lot of jargon at you. They have a lot of dazzling equipment and fancy tests. But the truth is, they know very little about the causes of these diseases.

There's powerful evidence that free radicals are the answer. But it may be years before establishment medicine accepts it.

You see, free radicals are easily neutralized by the antioxidants I told you about earlier — vitamin C, vitamin E, beta carotene, and others. And the medical industry has spent the last thirty years telling the public that vitamins are a waste of time.

Doctors know almost nothing about nutrition. They haven't studied it. Eventually, the medical establishment is going to adopt the free radical theory. Many doctors like myself already have.

In five years, everyone is going to be talking about the things you're learning in this book. The Nobel Prizes will be handed out to the people who are doing the research. Start to take advantage of the new health discoveries *now*. Don't wait until everybody's doing it. It may cost you your life to wait until the whole medical profession comes around.

There's something else I want to say

right now: Antioxidants are not drugs. They are *foods*. They have no toxic side effects. Since your body produces its own antioxidants all the time, you're just helping it do what comes naturally when you take more.

They can actually make you younger, as you'll see in the next chapter. . .

Chapter Three

How to Slow Down the "Aging Process"

"I'm glad to be here. I'm glad to be *anywhere*."
— George Burns, age 97

There are two aspects of the so-called "aging process." It's very important for you to understand the difference, because one of them can be controlled or even reversed. If you do so, there's no biological reason why you can't live to be 120.

The part of the aging process that can't be controlled involves the "biological clocks" that are built into our genes. Changes like puberty, menopause, and male pattern baldness are genetically programmed. In general, they can't be controlled — yet.

But most people don't die of these genetically-programmed changes. They die of cancer, stroke and heart disease largely caused by free radical damage. This is the part of the aging process that can be controlled or reversed.

Some of the research results are startling. In one experiment at the University of Ken-

tucky, scientists compared the ability of old
and young gerbils to run a complex maze. The
old gerbils made 2.5 times as many mistakes
as the young ones.

But when the elderly gerbils were
given a powerful antioxidant, they
were able to run the maze almost as
fast as the young gerbils.

It turns out that the old animals have
lower levels of key brain chemicals called
neurotransmitters. Their brain cells have
been damaged by free radicals. When they
take antioxidants, the neurotransmitter
levels rise markedly and the damaged brain
cells return almost to normal.

According to researchers, our free-radical
damage isn't programmed. It's mostly random, caused by a high-fat diet, stress, unhappiness, lack of exercise, smoking, pollution, chemicals, drugs, alcohol and a whole
variety of things that we can do something
about. If you can't break the bad habit, you
can neutralize it somewhat with antioxidants.

Until researchers started looking into
free radicals, nobody had any idea
why all this random damage occurred.
Scientists actually thought we might
have "suicide genes" or "suicide hor-

mones" set to go off. In other words, they thought all aging is programmed into our genes. Now we know better. A great deal of the damage is done by free radicals.

When you hear the average man or woman lives to be about 75, remember—those are averages.

You can live to be 110-120 years. And the extra years will be *good* years, not years in a hospital bed. This is fact, not conjecture. There's nothing "natural" about dying at 75. Scientists know that humans can live much, much longer if they don't succumb to free radical damage.

I don't know about you, but I enjoy the feeling that 120 is mine to try for. I used to believe that I wanted to be 120 and caught fleeing through a bedroom window. Now that I have someone to share my life with, I want to be 120 to walk with her on the beach, travel around the world, and just hold hands.

With the things we now know about health, you can actually pick a number between 75 and 120, aim for it. . .and there's a good chance you'll hit it!

Are you the sort of person who never exercises? You can still add years to your life by taking antioxidants.

Do you smoke and can't give it up?
Cheer up. The right supplements can
neutralize some of the bad effects of
smoking.

Sex life ain't what it used to be? There's
a lot you can do with supplements,
mild exercise and other techniques
I'll show you. Just getting off blood
pressure and cholesterol-lowering
drugs may solve the problem.

You see, you don't have to do everything
right. There are dozens of different things
you can do. Each and every one of them will
make you feel better and more energetic.
Each will reduce your odds of heart attack,
stroke, or cancer. You can even reverse
wrinkling in your skin.

Listen, a group of 90-year-old men and
women who lifted weights for eight weeks
nearly tripled the strength of their arms and
legs. Under medical supervision, these ten
nursing home residents lifted weights three
times a week. They were able to go from
lifting about 15 pounds to lifting over 40.

Two of them no longer required canes.
One of them could get up out of a chair
without using his arms — something
he couldn't do before the weight lift-

ing. These people were in *their nineties*. And the program was *only eight weeks*.

You see, there are a lot of things we can do to become happier and healthier. They aren't secret. It's just that most people don't do them.

You decide how much you want to do and when you want to do it. But I'll make you a bet: After you've found out what it's like to feel better, you'll want to do more, not less. The terms of my bet are simple: Just try my monthly newsletter *Healthy Longevity*. If you try just one of my techniques, and you don't feel better in 90 days, I'll send you a full refund (order form on page 121).

I want you to know something very important. . .

The things most people eat and the way they live are not good indications of how long *you* can live.

The cancer and heart disease rates affecting most people do not represent how much *you* are at risk.

If you eliminate random free-radical damage or repair it, you could live a healthy life to the end of your genetically determined life span, probably around 110 to 120 years.

During the 1980s, scientists discovered a strain of bacteria that could survive the lethal environment of radioactive waste water. One of the ways radioactivity kills most forms of life, including bacteria, is by releasing cascades of free radicals.

But this particular bacterium generated high levels of antioxidants — as much as fifty times more than other bacteria — and was able to survive radiation.

Think about that: *A high level of antioxidants enabled these bacteria to survive the equivalent of nuclear fallout from an atomic war!*

In humans, we now know that heart disease is caused by atherosclerosis (hardening of the arteries). Every 34 seconds an American dies of this disease. Taken as a whole, the disease costs the nation at least $110 billion per year.

Your doctor will tell you high cholesterol causes athersclerosis, but that's only half the story. The medical profession is at least five years behind on this.

They used to believe all cholesterol is bad. Then they figured out that only one type of cholesterol — LDL — is bad, but they still haven't got the whole story.

The research shows clogging of the arteries is actually caused by LDL that's gone "rancid" because it's attacked by free radicals. When ___ goes bad it becomes a free rad___ itself and attacks other cells. Eventually the chain reaction affects all the arteries.

A study published by the American Heart Association reports that large doses of vitamin E can prevent free radical damage to LDL — the "bad" cholesterol. Alternative-care doctors like myself believe that this is precisely the mechanism that causes atherosclerosis.

According to the AHA, "Recent research indicates that so-called 'bad' LDL cholesterol undergoes oxidation, similar to butter becoming rancid, when exposed to certain toxic particles called oxygen free radicals. This 'oxidized' LDL seems to promote atherosclerosis, the buildup of fatty plaque in the walls of arteries."

That's exactly what I've been saying.

So do these powerful, arch-conservative organizations now tell people to take vitamins E, C, A and other antioxidants? Are the National Cancer Institute and the American Heart Association finally getting on board? Incredibly, no.

The head of the AHA's nutrition committee says, "Until scientists determine the correct doses of these vitamins and whether they actually provide any protection, people who buy vitamin pills may be wasting their money." At present, he adds, the AHA has no plans to recommend the use of antioxidant vitamins.

My friend, I want you to get this straight: There is impressive evidence that antioxidants prevent cancer, stroke and heart disease. They are natural nutrients found in food. They are known to be harmless even in huge doses.

And the medical establishment is hanging back.

I don't know about you, but I'm not waiting to take these life giving supplements. There are problems with our medical system. *Big* problems. Let me tell you more. . .

Chapter Four

The Problem With Most Doctors

The August 31 *Wall Street Journal* carried an article that says a lot about the medical establishment.

The article dealt with 25,000 victims of a very stupid type of surgery. They had their jaw joints replaced with an artificial jaw that doesn't work. The manufacturer has now gone out of business and the FDA has seized all its products.

Medical experts now expect all or most of those artificial joints to break up into tiny fragments. That causes what's left of the natural jawbone to erode.

"This isn't my face," says one of the victims. "I used to be real pretty." She's now had eight operations that have left her disfigured, without jaw joints, her mouth permanently hanging open.

Alone at night, says the *Wall Street Journal*, she can hardly bear the muscle spasms and the pain. "It never goes away; it's God-awful pain," says the woman.

The 25,000 people who submitted to this surgery suffered from something called TMJ syndrome. TMJ stands for your lower jaw joint, called the temporo-mandibular joint.

It is an incredibly delicate, complicated living thing. It lets you move your lower jaw up and down and side to side as you speak, bite, chew, swallow, smile, laugh, or frown.

For many people something goes terribly wrong with their TMJ. The muscle goes into spasm, the bones grind against one another. The victim can suffer from unbelievable headaches, earaches, jaw and facial pain.

If you've never suffered from TMJ syndrome, it's hard to imagine the pain. It's as intense as a migraine headache. So it's no wonder those 25,000 people were willing to try surgery.

There's just one problem: TMJ syndrome is caused by stress. It happens to people who are so anxious, worried and unhappy they grind their teeth in their sleep. There's nothing wrong with their jaws. There's something wrong with their lives.

It's often called the "yuppie disease" because it usually happens to overworked, stressed-out young professionals.

Twenty years ago, nobody had even *heard* of TMJ syndrome. It's caused by the way we live.

The *Wall Street Journal* says, "Compounding the [surgical] tragedy, new research in the Netherlands suggests that the best treatment for TMJ may be none at all, because most TMJ disorders abate in a few years."

I can do even better than that. Come to my office for an hour and I can teach you relaxation techniques. In a couple of weeks, you can control the problem yourself. Then after you leave my office, go to a good massage therapist and you'll be on your way to recovery.

No drugs. No surgery.

Have you ever gone to a doctor with headaches, backache, TMJ syndrome? Did he tell you about massage therapy? Or something called "biofeedback?" If not, shame on him.

More likely, your doctor will prescribe "muscle relaxants" or some other drugs. You might feel better for a few weeks, but don't count on even that much. And for sure it won't work long-term. Your body will continue to deteriorate. The drugs will actually speed up the overall deterioration of your health. Next thing you know he'll be talking about surgery.

You might wonder how 25,000 people

could be implanted with an artificial joint that doesn't work.

Aren't these things carefully tested? Hasn't the FDA or some other government agency approved these things?

When it comes to surgical procedures, the answer is often *no*. It's likely that no government agency has approved the surgical technique the doctor wants to use on you. No studies prove that procedures like prostate surgery, coronary bypass, balloon angioplasty, or radical mastectomy (breast removal) actually work.

There are studies that show they *don't* work.

The company that made the jaw implants did no human or animal trials.

Stories like the jaw implant make me extremely sad, but I also have to admit that I was part of the problem — until I "went straight." I'd like to tell you about it in the next chapter.

Chapter Five

Confessions of an Ex-Surgeon

I performed about 2,000 coronary by-pass operations before I finally figured out I wasn't helping people. I haven't picked up a scalpel since 1981, but I've saved more patients than I did as a surgeon.

I'm able to help more people because I decided to get into a different line of work:

Instead of treating illness, I help people stay healthy.

Let me show you what I mean. . .

A 56-year-old nurse entered my program a few years ago. Her history was very simple. She had suffered from high blood pressure for twenty years, weighed 185 pounds, and had 35% body fat.

She was taking three medications to control her blood pressure. She was taking another medication, Diabenase, to control a case of diabetes that was brought on by the blood pressure medications.

And she was taking a fifth medication

for heart failure.

Three months after entering my program, she was down to 160 pounds. She no longer had to take the diabetes and heart failure pills. She was able to drop two of the blood pressure prescriptions and reduce the dose on the third to half of what she'd been taking.

After 20 years of diabetes, she had it controlled within three months.

It wasn't my doing. I was just there to give advice. She did it herself. That is what can happen when you take control of your own fate by seeking *alternatives* to drugs and surgery.

This particular patient had to tell her physician that she was entering our program. He told her it was a waste of time. But the program *did* work. She saved a lot of money on medical bills and greatly reduced her risk of stroke or heart attack.

Her doctor meant well, but his attitude is typical of our medical system.

- They "know" that vitamin and mineral supplements don't work.

- They "know" surgery and radiation are the best treatments for breast cancer and prostate cancer.

- They "know" that if you have high blood pressure you'll have to take medication for the rest of your life.

- They "know" bypass surgery or balloon angioplasty is the best treatment for blocked arteries.

Those "medical facts" and a whole lot more are *false*. What's more, they aren't isolated medical mistakes. They represent a whole way of looking at things that is wrong.

I'm a medical doctor and I used to look at things the same way as the medical establishment. Basically, their view is that the body is a sort of machine you fix when it breaks down. I shucked off this dangerous, mistaken point of view and learned how human beings really work.

Over the past 40 years, evidence has been piling up that the way the body works is totally different from what the medical profession thinks.

Thousands of other doctors all over the United States are doing the same thing I'm doing. We are painfully "unlearning" all the myths we used to believe. The old way of looking at things is under assault. The walls are crumbling.

I really think the key to preventing cancer, heart disease, stroke and arthritis is within our grasp.

If you get nothing else out of this book, I want you to get this: *You* control how healthy you are. *You* control how long you are going to live.

Take a moment and imagine something that's heavy for you, like a bag of groceries, a bag of topsoil, or maybe a tire. Now imagine that you can pick it up and swing it around like a feather.

Imagine that you fall asleep at night promptly, doze six or eight hours without interruption, and get up feeling fresh, rested, and eager to get going.

Imagine looking as good as you did fifteen years ago — and feeling better!

You can do it.

It really is possible to feel good all the time. It's up to you. Don't wait until you are desperately sick and then expect the doctor to cut you open and replace the parts, or fix you up with a miracle drug. Those things don't work.

As I said earlier, my aim is to put myself out of business. The happiest day of my life is when a patient doesn't need me anymore.

I have a lot of happy days now — far more than I had as a surgeon and pill-pusher. I'll have another one — if you read this book and tell me you've changed just one thing about your life.

I don't want you to change a lot of things. People who try to do everything at once often end up doing nothing, after a few months.

I'd like you to start by doing *just one thing*.

And I want you to do that one thing until it comes naturally.

You're in luck, too, because there's a very easy way to get started: antioxidant vitamins and minerals.

This book is going to give you a "menu" of other things you can do, so you can pick the ones that appeal to you. Just do whatever is easiest. You will learn. . .

- A way to lose weight without giving up any of your favorite foods.

- How to eliminate 75% to 80% of all visits to a doctor.

- The number one factor that can predict heart attacks. (No, it's *not* smoking, cholesterol, obesity, or blood pressure.)

- How to control your own blood pressure.

- The dangers that lurk in our drinking water.

And much more.

There's a lot to cover, so let's keep going!

Chapter Six

You Can't Be a Bigger Mess Than I Was

I lost my faith in the medical establishment because I was a full-fledged member of it and I could see it wasn't working.

I received my medical degree at the University of Missouri. Then I received my training in surgery as a resident at the University of Michigan Medical Center. This was a very tough program to get into — only 24 young doctors were admitted. It was even tougher to *stay* in. Sixteen of the 24 were asked to leave because they didn't meet the program's high standards.

As one of the eight survivors I completed my training in thoracic and cardiovascular surgery and became a heart surgeon. This was in the Sixties, when open heart surgery was first introduced. I witnessed some of the first open heart operations in history. It was intensely exciting.

Many patients died on the operating

table in those early days. But we believed in
what we were doing. These patients were at
the end of the rope, and surgery seemed to be
the best answer. Besides, our whole medical
approach was "open the hood and fix 'er up."
That's what we were taught.

After the University of Michigan I went
to South Dakota, where I developed the only
open heart surgical program in the state. In
fact, I was the only Board Certified cardiac
surgeon in the state.

Problem is, my patients were dying.

I performed about 2,000 coronary bypass
operations. A great many of my patients were
back on the operating table within three to
five years — or dead. At some hospitals — not
mine, thank God — more than one patient
out of ten dies.

Even for those who get "well," life is
never the same. Open heart surgery is a
major trauma. It's a horrible thing to go
through. If you have friends who have gone
through it, you may notice they are often
depressed and have trouble remembering
things. I've seen strong people become weak
and dependent.

> **Let me take a "time out" and say it
> again: You don't have to go
> through this. It is totally unnec-
> essary. You can "fix" yourself.**

I know, because I did it. While I was a big-shot heart surgeon, my weight drifted up to 225 pounds. I smoked a pack-and-a-half a day. I ate anything I could get my hands on, and had two or three drinks whenever I didn't have patients to care for.

I would spend hours in surgery reaming out big long yellow sausages of fatty material from people's arteries. Then I'd waddle my 225 pounds over to the cafeteria and have a cheeseburger, fries and cheesecake!

Looking back, I can't believe it. What did I think all that yellow gook was that I was taking out of other people's arteries?

I was in my thirties then. Now I'm 52. I feel and look better than I did then. If I had stayed on the same course, I would now have heart disease, high blood pressure, ulcers and probably alcoholism.

Elmer's Glue in the Arteries

Let me tell you a story about a blood sample that was taken from a very nice man who was extremely overweight. Normally, when you draw a blood sample and let it sit for an hour, it separates into two parts. A transparent yellow serum rises to the top — you can see through it — and the heavy matter settles to the bottom.

But this guy's blood was like white

glue. It was thick and greasy — it even stuck to the sides of the test tube. It turns out the guy had had a cheese-burger and a milk shake before he came to the hospital.

You see, when you eat a meal like that there's a surge of fat in the blood. It takes your body about four hours to clear it out. That was the "Elmer's glue" stuff in the test tube. It's a well-known phenomenon called lypemia, meaning fat in the blood.

A patient like that can expect to be back on the operating table within three to five years — or dead. And what about the rest of his arteries? The disease affects your whole body, not just the heart arteries.

100% Success Rate Without Surgery

In 1977, I got tired of this and tried something else. If I had a patient who suf-fered pain in the legs because of clogged arteries ("claudication"), I make a deal with him. Instead of surgery, I'd tell him, "Do some mild exercise, and give up smoking for a year. If your legs are still in pain, *then* I'll operate."

One hundred patients took me up on the bet. And not one of them needed surgery a year later.

I'll tell you something that really shook me up. I was set to do a triple bypass on a 72-year-old man. When we got him into the operating room, we found out he needed *five* bypasses, but his arteries were so hard we couldn't cut them with a scalpel!

We sewed him up again without doing the bypasses. I thought it was hopeless, but I hated to say so to his wife. So I told her the man should try exercise and change his diet.

Six months later he was farming again. And 12 months later he was off all medications and suffered no chest pain.

That was in 1977. I got a letter from the man in 1988. He was still alive, still farming part-time, still not on medication. He walked four miles a day.

If you want to live long, that's the kind of treatment that works. What the typical doctor recommends is all wet. Let me show you what I mean. . .

Chapter Seven

The Clogged Drain Approach

If you have heart disease you'll probably never know it. For most victims, the first heart attack is the last one. Each year, about 750,000 Americans suffer a heart attack, but only 250,000 survive.

If you are "lucky," and your heart disease is discovered in time, chances are your doctor will recommend something called balloon angioplasty.

This is the current "gee whiz" technique. Since 1978, it has pushed aside bypass surgery as the favorite procedure. It is cheaper, easier for the doctor, and not so hard on the patient.

Problem is, six times as many angioplasty patients need repeat treatment or surgery as those who had a bypass.

In angioplasty, a tiny balloon is threaded through your blocked arteries and expanded. Supposedly this clears the heart arteries by pushing the fatty "plaque" against the artery wall.

Some people call this the "clogged drain"

theory of treating heart disease.

Whatever you call it, it's big business. My colleagues perform about 300,000 angioplasties a year at an average cost of $14,000. That's $4.2 billion right there, not including drugs and follow-up.

A 1992 study in the *Journal of the American Medical Association* found that half the angioplasties carried out in the U.S. were probably unnecessary. According to the study, ". . .not a single properly randomized study supports the superior advantage, if any, of angioplasty as compared with medical therapy . . ."

> The American College of Cardiologists asks, "Is angioplasty being done for cardiologists or for patients?"

The kindest thing I can say about angioplasty is that it's a short-term solution. *Studies show the arteries close up again in 57% of all cases.* And the terrified patient has to undergo another angioplasty. If he or she lives through all this, bypass surgery is next (average cost: $43,000).

I'm not a fan of drug therapy, but studies show even drugs are a better treatment than either angioplasty *or* bypass.

Another "gee whiz" technique will eventually replace angioplasty. Next you'll hear about "laser endarterectomy." There's also something called "atherectomy" (I call it the Roto-Rooter). They actually insert a tiny, high-speed rotating knife in your artery to cut away the cholesterol.

Let me tell you something: One out of 12 atherectomy patients dies within six months, according to two studies. Within six months, the arteries close up again in about half of all atherectomy patients.

> I'm having a 99% success rate with people who have been told they need angioplasty or coronary bypass. Remember the guy who was still farming years later? He's not an exception. He represents what anyone can do.

The answer to the aging diseases is quite different from what modern medicine thinks. . .

Chapter Eight

Start Losing Weight Today Without Changing a Thing You Eat

I didn't write this book to rag you about smoking or being overweight. I know it's not easy to change. Remember, I used to smoke and be overweight myself.

It's not my idea to put you on *my* diet and *my* exercise program. You won't stick with it for more than a few months. You know it and I know it.

My approach is to help you pick things you are willing to do and then do them — one at a time. Obviously, it's easier to get started on the food supplements. I don't want you to do everything at once. The idea is for you to tailor a program to yourself. . . a program that fits *you*.

Subscribing to my monthly 12-page newsletter — *Healthy Longevity* — is the best way for you to *gradually* change your habits until you feel good all the time. That way, I can chat with you every month. Subscription information is on page 121.

> But meanwhile, you can start to feel better and lose weight without changing a single thing in your diet. All you have to do is change the *way* you eat.

They may not know it, but many over-weight people use food to comfort themselves when they are depressed, lonely, or anxious. People also use food as a stimulant. It's a sort of "turn-on." Yet their brains never get the message that they've had enough. They don't even enjoy their food. So it takes more and more to make them feel satisfied.

You can get more pleasure from your food, feel totally satisfied, and yet eat less. It's very simple. Just try the following. . .

(1) Always sit down when you eat, prefer-ably at a table. Don't eat while standing, driving, walking, or talking on the phone.

(2) Don't read or watch television while you eat. Don't even listen to music.

(3) Eat only when your stomach is empty.

Usually, this means about four hours after the last meal.

(4) Don't take a bite until you've swallowed the previous bite. This may sound obvious. But just observe people and you'll see them stuffing additional forkfuls into their mouths — which are already full of mush — and talking at the same time.

(5) Don't eat when you're not hungry. Again, this may sound obvious, but many people eat past the point where they are full. Before taking a second helping, wait five minutes. That's about how much time it takes your stomach to let your brain know it's had enough. After five minutes, chances are you won't feel hungry anymore — even though you craved a second helping just moments ago.

On the other hand, you'll experience some discomfort if you eat more than you need. You'll feel tired and sleepy after a meal. If you eat a lot more than you need, you'll actually feel sick.

Have you ever dined in a restaurant where you had a strong craving for dessert, but you had to pay the check and leave because there was no time? If you are like most people, the craving for dessert probably passes after you're out on the street or in your car. You forget you were "still hungry." In fact, you feel quite full.

I have a simple suggestion: Observe the same thing at home. Wait five minutes, and you'll probably find out you are satisfied.

If you take these five simple steps for one week, I predict you'll feel better. You'll have more energy. You'll want to keep eating this way because you're *enjoying* your food as you never have before.

If you have a weight problem, stay with this easy program. I predict you'll start to lose weight. You will get up from the table completely satisfied. Yet you'll be eating less.

You can lose a couple of pounds a month without giving up anything. That wouldn't be so bad, would it?

Now, if a "regular doctor" heard me tell you that, he'd probably yell "quack!" In the next chapter, I'm going to tell you who the real quacks are.

Chapter Nine

They Call It Science?

My fellow medical doctors pride themselves on being "scientific." Other approaches like chiropractic or acupuncture are "nonscientific." In fact, your M.D. will probably call those people quacks.

"Quack" is the ugliest insult you can throw at someone in the health field. It's like a schoolboy saying something about your mother.

In all honesty, I have to tell you that conventional medicine is not very scientific. Take something like ultrasound imaging, or sonograms. This procedure takes a little picture of a fetus while it's still in the womb. The sonogram may end up in the family photo album as baby's first picture, *but it's completely unnecessary and may even be dangerous*.

Studies show ultrasound produces cell damage. One doctor wrote, "I'd look for possible behavioral changes — in reflexes, IQ, attention span." A 1984 study showed higher dyslexia among children who'd been exposed to ultrasound in the womb.

There are nine studies of ultrasound testing during labor and birth. *Every study shows this procedure produces a worse outcome for mother and child.* Yet fetal monitors continue to be used in almost every delivery room.

Recently there was an article in the *New England Journal of Medicine* — the bible of the medical profession. It says sonograms are not needed during pregnancy unless there is good reason to believe there may be a problem with the baby.

The study involved 15,000 women who were *not* high risk. Half received routine sonograms and half did not. The number of babies born with complications was the same in both groups. The number of premature babies was the same in both groups. The number of low-birth-weight babies was the same in both groups.

Why do we do this test?

The FDA, the American Medical Association and the American College of Obstetrics and Gynecology all say pregnant women should not receive routine sonograms, but doctors do them anyway. And we all pay for it, over one billion dollars a year, according to *The Wall Street Journal*. It's a sorry waste of money and a threat to health.

The Poison In Your Mouth

Medical doctors are not the only ones who take this stubborn, head-in-the-sand approach. Chances are, your dentist does the same thing when it comes to those silver fillings in your mouth.

Silver fillings are actually an amalgam of several materials including mercury, a deadly toxin. The American Dental Association insists the mercury is harmless. They say it never gets out of the filling. They are wrong.

A study from the University of Calgary Department of Medicine proves that mercury vapor gets out of the fillings and finds its way into your body tissue.

Tests done on sheep proved that large quantities of mercury quickly migrated from the fillings to the kidneys, liver, stomach, intestines and lungs. There was a 5% reduction in kidney function a month after the fillings were placed. In pregnant animals the mercury got into the fetus.

A University of Georgia study using monkeys showed the mercury got into the intestine and altered the bacteria there. Mercury was detected in the gut only two weeks after the fillings were placed. The researchers believe the mercury may be responsible for allergies and yeast infections. It appears the mercury gives rise to bacteria that antibiotics can't kill.

Out of 1600 people who had their fillings removed, 89% said their allergies or digestive problems were cured or got better. (Note: Don't have your fillings removed until I give you more information in my newsletter, *Healthy Longevity*. But meanwhile don't let your dentist put in any more mercury fillings. Safe fillings are now available. Insist on them, no matter what he says.)

Cut First, Ask Questions Later

Remember what I told you about TMJ syndrome, balloon angioplasty and heart bypasses? Well that's just the tip of the iceberg. From sea to shining sea, people in this country are being cut open for no good reason.

Take breast surgery. If they find a lump in the breast, most doctors will perform a radical mastectomy — the entire breast is removed, along with the surrounding chest muscles, soft tissues, and all the lymph nodes as far as the armpit. It is every woman's nightmare — for good reason.

Radical mastectomy was introduced a hundred years ago.

Yet there has never been a single study showing the operation is better than just removing the

lump or removing only the breast while not removing the surrounding tissue.

Those are the three choices. Removing the lump is called lumpectomy and removing only the breast is called a simple mastectomy. Radical mastectomy is like using an H-bomb where a bullet would do.

Despite all the evidence, radical mastectomy has an iron grip on the minds of surgeons. Nearly fifty years ago, an Illinois study showed no difference in five- and ten-year survival rates for radical mastectomy, lumpectomy and simple mastectomy.

In 1969, a British study of 8,000 cases showed the same thing again.

Studies in the 1980s showed the same thing again.

Through all of this, most surgeons continued to do radical mastectomies. In 1990, the National Institute of Health advised doctors to perform the less damaging surgery when the tumor is smaller than 4 cm. and chest muscle and skin are not involved.

Guess what: Most doctors still don't offer that option to their patients.

Would the real quacks please stand up?

Doctors Do Good Things, Too

I've said some harsh words. So let me

just say that the medical profession — my profession — has done a huge amount of good. If you break a bone, or you have appendicitis, or you want to avoid catching polio, run to the nearest M.D.

If I were injured in a car accident I wouldn't think of going to anyone but an M.D. If I contract a bacterial disease like pneumonia or TB I definitely want antibiotics — by prescription, from an M.D.

When I first started in heart surgery, we did a booming business operating on the hearts of folks in their twenties and thirties. Their heart valves were falling apart because they had suffered from rheumatic fever when they were children.

Now rheumatic fever practically doesn't exist, thanks to modern medicine. Those open heart operations aren't needed anymore.

And modern medicine has also eliminated smallpox from the whole world. It's a disease that doesn't exist anymore.

Those are some of the things doctors have accomplished.

And I'm proud to be a doctor.

But the big killers of our time — heart disease, stroke, and cancer — are largely "lifestyle diseases." They are caused by the way we live — especially the food we eat. . .or don't eat. They are caused by toxins and pollution in our environment. Lack of exercise and even lack of happiness are also factors. The most effective way of fighting them is to take the antioxidants I described earlier. But that is not the only answer.

Do you know the number one risk factor for heart disease?

It's not smoking. It's not high cholesterol. It's not high blood pressure.

The number one risk factor is whether you are unhappy.

As I hope you are starting to see, the medical establishment is seriously on the wrong track where these modern diseases are concerned.

Yet these are the things most people suffer from. These things probably account for at least 80% of visits to doctors' offices.

> *You can eliminate 80% of your visits to your doctor.*

Turn to the next chapter, and let me give you a good example.

Chapter Ten

Lower Your Blood Pressure Without Drugs

A person with high blood pressure may typically be taking three or four medications. One pill causes the blood vessels to dilate (open up), thereby lowering blood pressure. But the drug also causes the heart to speed up. So the doctor prescribes a second drug to slow down the heart.

One of these two drugs may cause fluid retention, so the doctor prescribes a third medication — a diuretic or "water pill."

My friend, these drugs are real doozies. Almost all hypertension drugs cause impotence in males. Diuretics can cause dizziness and depression, even headaches. They can also cause your body to lose valuable minerals and actually *raise* your cholesterol levels.

Another class of blood pressure drug called "beta blockers" may cause depression, hallucinations, insomnia, liver and kidney damage. If you smoke or have any kind of respiratory problem — even hay fever allergies — beta blockers are dangerous.

In a survey published in the *New England Journal of Medicine*, only 48% of patients felt that blood pressure medication had improved their lives. And 98% of their friends and relatives reported that the patient's quality of life had gotten worse!

Your blood pressure may still be high, even with all these drugs. Your doctor may keep you on the drugs anyway because it's the "approved treatment" and he needs to cover his hindquarters from lawsuits.

It's a shame so many people are taking these medicines. The fact is that 75% to 90% of all patients have only mild hypertension! They don't need any drugs at all.

What Is High Blood Pressure?

Doctors don't agree among themselves on what constitutes high blood pressure. One doctor will give you a drug for 140/90 blood pressure, another doctor will not.

The second doctor is right. 140/90 is not that high, especially for someone over 50. If the second number, called the "diastolic pressure," is under 110, I seldom prescribe a drug.

I prefer to treat "borderline hypertension" with diet, relaxation techniques, and a half-hour walk every evening. (You don't

want to take walks? Well, that's your choice.
The other techniques may do the job. But
even a little bit of exercise is extremely
valuable. A University of Connecticut study
shows dramatic drops in blood pressure from
a leisurely half hour walk.)

The antioxidants — vitamins C, E, A,
selenium and zinc — are a must because
hardening of the arteries has been traced to
free radical damage.

Potassium and magnesium supplements
can also help. Recent studies show that men
who consume more magnesium in their diet
had consistently lower blood pressure. That
was the finding in a study by the State University of New York in Brooklyn.

Does Your Doctor Make You Nervous?

There's also the problem of "white coat"
blood pressure. Let's face it: A doctor's office
is not very cozy or friendly in most cases. You
may be one of the people who see their blood
pressure skyrocket the minute a nurse slips
on the cuff.

If you're having your blood pressure
taken in a doctor's office, first of all just *notice*
if you feel uptight. Being aware of the problem can help you calm down. If your blood
pressure registers high, insist that the doctor

or nurse test it again after you've relaxed a
few minutes. Use the time to close your eyes
and take a few deep breaths. If possible, read
the comics in your newspaper or the joke
pages in *Reader's Digest*.

If you can lower your blood pressure
with these simple techniques, congratula-
tions! You are on your way to mastering
biofeedback. That's a fancy word for learning
to listen to what your body is telling you.

If your doctor *still* tells you that your
blood pressure is too high, monitor your own
blood pressure at home. Sears, Wal-Mart and
your own drugstore sell cheap, simple de-
vices for taking your own blood pressure. For
a fraction of what you spend on drugs, you
might find out that you are only suffering
from "white coat" hypertension.

When you monitor your own blood pressure, you may also find it's high only at
certain times and places — like when you're
at work! If so, your problem is stress.

Many people have actually lowered their
own blood pressure by home-monitoring. This
is do-it-yourself biofeedback. In a study of
high blood pressure patients, 43% were able
to reduce their blood pressure by ten points
or more just by measuring it themselves
twice a day for a month.

You see, these things are under your
control. More on this in the next chapter. . .

Chapter Eleven

A Tale of Two Women

I'd like to tell you the story of two women I know. They are both 78.

The first one is tormented with arthritis pain, day and night. She's had surgery half a dozen times in the last 15 years, and she's still in constant pain. Now the doctors say they won't operate anymore.

She's on three medications for high blood pressure. She has several more prescriptions for the arthritis pain. She has stomach pain from all the arthritis "pain-killers."

She is losing her vision. And also her memory. She's crabby and loses her temper over every little thing. Nobody says it out loud, but she and the people who love her know she only has a few years left.

The other woman is also 78. She just got married again and took a honeymoon on a lovely tropical island.

She's not taking any medication. Her heart is fine.

She drives her own car, does her own shopping, and keeps a beautiful garden. She even plays a little golf.

At family gatherings, she's the joy of her children, grandchildren, and (soon) great-grandchildren. Everyone loves to be around her.

What's the difference between these two women? Why is one vibrant, healthy and happy while the other is sick and miserable?

That's what this little book is all about.

Some people will tell you it's all in the genes, or maybe one woman had a better doctor, or maybe it's just luck. They will tell you that getting heart disease or arthritis is like being struck by lightning. Some people get hit, some don't. There's no use thinking about it.

I don't believe that. I know it's not true, because every day I work with people who are preventing the "lifestyle diseases."

There's a lot you can do to make sure you end up like the second woman and not like the first one. You can start today. And the most powerful tools are actually the easiest ones to use.

What's more, it doesn't matter what age you are. You can start making the right choices now. Even the first woman can experience dramatic improvement in her health and happiness. This book is showing you how. My monthly newsletter, *Healthy*

Longevity will show you even more.

I'm not saying genes or luck have nothing to do with health. But there is a lot more you can do for yourself than you probably think. The first thing you need to do is take advantage of the *nutrition revolution*.

There's overwhelming research — thousands of studies — to show vitamins, minerals and other supplements can help prevent cancer, heart disease, high blood pressure and arthritis. Often, they can reverse damage that's already been done. They can make you smarter, happier and more energetic. You can even make your muscles stronger just by taking a food supplement.

Pamper Yourself

That's right: Pamper yourself.

Many people watch themselves fall apart in slow motion. Many young people in their twenties already suffer from headaches and tummy trouble, especially if they have job and family pressure. (And who doesn't?)

In their thirties and forties they begin to experience back or joint pain. They get a "spare tire" around the middle. Their skin becomes dry and wrinkled. They feel tired all the time.

One fine day, their doctor tells them they have high blood pressure or high cholesterol. Chances are he puts them on medication.

Chances are, the medication causes fatigue, depression, impotence or other problems.

One fine day, you wake up and you're old.

It doesn't have to happen. In fact, it should *not* happen.

This isn't natural. It's not an "aging process" caused by an "aging gene." It is slow self-destruction by bad food, stress, and lack of exercise.

It can't be fixed by antacids for the stomach, pain-killers for back pain or headaches, "water pills" for the blood pressure, moisturizers for the dry skin, crash diets for the weight problem.

All those things only treat *symptoms*. They don't get at the root of the problem. Modern medicine is big on treating symptoms, especially when it comes to the lifestyle diseases — the diseases that account for 80% of visits to your doctor.

Pain-killers, for example, are handed out like M&Ms for headache, backache and arthritis. They don't do a thing for the underlying condition. All a pain-killer does is cut the communication between your brain and the part that hurts. The pain is still there, but your conscious mind is not picking up the phone and listening. Meanwhile, the condition gets worse.

The way to cure diseases like hardening of the arteries, cancer, diabetes, arthritis, fatigue and high blood pressure is this: Figure out the root cause of the problem — diet, lack of exercise, stress — and change it. But please remember — don't change your whole life at once. Do one thing at a time.

Pamper yourself. Start treating yourself like someone who is worth keeping around for 120 years. Figure out how you are mistreating yourself and stop it.

Don't Believe Death Sentences

Learn to be skeptical of doctors who tell you nothing can be done about aging and the lifestyle diseases. Their view is a lot of hooey, given what we know about free radicals.

Personally, I would never tell you a condition is hopeless — including the "aging process." For one thing, research clearly shows that just giving a person *hope* strengthens the immune system and helps fight off disease. For another thing, research shows the lifestyle diseases can be controlled through supplements, diet, exercise and relaxation.

I know of a Maryland woman who has multiple sclerosis. That's what three different doctors told her. They also told her there was nothing they could do.

Not willing to give up, this woman went to a doctor who believed in good, healthy food. Working with him for several months, she found out that sulfites — a very common preservative — brought on her MS attacks.

Now she feels much stronger. She's alert. She's energetic. Her vision is fine. When she eats anything containing sulfites she gets sick. When she avoids sulfites, she feels much better. It's that simple.

That's what I mean by pampering yourself.

The woman with MS can't eat potato chips, or Twinkies or soft drinks anymore. But she feels *good*.

There was another woman who was told she had "incurable" MS. Like most victims, she was told the condition would steadily get worse. But she had heard about the dangers of mercury fillings, and she decided to have hers removed, since nothing else offered any hope.

After having the fillings out, she left the dentist's office using a cane and leaning on a friend. The next day, she threw away her cane. And the day after that she went dancing!

You're the Guinea Pig

You see, for sixty years or more we've been conducting a vast experiment on ourselves. The fillings, drugs, food additives, pesticides and even the chlorine and fluoride in our water may have lethal effects. They may affect one person and not another, one community but not the town five miles down the road.

We don't have much idea of how these things affect our health, but evidence is now starting to pour in. As with mercury fillings, most of the news is bad. We're suffering from diseases that didn't exist a hundred years ago.

Did you know the first reported heart attack occurred in 1896? Gives you a different perspective on the problem, doesn't it? There are dozens of countries where the disease that kills nearly a million Americans a year is not even in the top 10 causes of death.

Dr. Paul Dudley White, a famous heart specialist a generation ago, said, "When I graduated from medical school in 1911, I had never heard of coronary thrombosis [heart attack]. . ."

But the good news is you can often figure out what's making you sick and get it out of your life. You *can* take charge of your own health. And you can get help from the new breed of doctors who are open to the new way of looking at health.

Unlike establishment doctors, we don't pretend to have all the answers. But we're willing to look at everything.

In the next chapter, I want to give you a very simple way to begin taking charge.

Chapter Twelve

Don't Drink the Water!

Stop drinking the water that comes out of your tap. Drink bottled water, or better yet buy a home water purifier. It's one of the easiest things you can do to add years to your life.

Chlorine is in almost everybody's tap water. This chemical effectively kills the little water-borne critters that cause typhoid, cholera and dysentery.

Problem is, chlorinated drinking water is directly responsible for more than 4,200 cases of bladder cancer and 6,500 cases of rectal cancer every year.

Those figures are based on a study published in the *American Journal of Public Health* (AJPH) just a couple of years ago. Frankly, I wasn't surprised. I had stopped drinking tap water long ago and urged my patients to do the same.

You see, chlorine reacts with other substances in water to form chloroform, carbon tetrachloride and other cancer-causing compounds (carcinogens). Understand this: These are well-known carcinogens.

There's nothing speculative about this. The only question is whether there is enough in your water to be harmful.

For years, researchers have tried to find out if we're getting harmful amounts of these compounds in our water, but they were never able to reach a firm conclusion.

The AJPH study, conducted by the Medical College of Milwaukee, drew together all the other studies. That way the authors had enough data to show a definite link between chlorinated water and cancer.

> This points up the danger of waiting until scientists are "sure" about something. More than a hundred thousand people came down with cancer in the last decade from this carcinogen. But I guarantee if you ask your doctor even today he'll tell you there's nothing to worry about.

There's a new technology, using ozone, that is much better than chlorine for killing microorganisms. Los Angeles and a few other places already employ ozone, but it's likely to be decades before it reaches the rest of the nation. The money isn't there to switch every water system over to ozone.

No problem: *It's very easy to filter your water at home or buy bottled water. There's no reason to spend your whole life drinking a chemical whose effects are uncertain, hoping there's no harm in it.*

The EPA (Environmental Protection Agency) knows there's a chlorine problem but they figure the benefit of preventing typhoid and the other diseases outweighs the cancer risk. Kill the bugs and take your chances on the tumors.

That's fine and dandy as long as you're not one of the 10,000 people who get cancer this year!

The EPA has also learned that chlorinated drinking water decreases the "good" cholesterol (HDL) and increases the bad cholesterol (LDL). So you increase your heart disease risk and your cancer risk at the same time.

Chlorine Doesn't Get All the Bugs

Quite a few disease-causing organisms are resistant to chlorine, including the one that causes Legionnaire's disease. Nearly every outbreak of this disease since 1982 has been traced to a water system.

The EPA knows that contaminated water has made 140,000 people ill in the U.S. since 1971. They've identified 570 instances of contamination. Experts believe 25 times as many people *don't* report their illnesses.

Your greatest risk is if you live in a small

town. Small water systems that serve fewer than 3,300 people simply don't have the money to keep pace. Over 90% of the systems in violation of EPA standards are small .

But even big cities aren't completely safe. Last April, thousands of Milwaukee residents became sick from a chlorine-resistant bug called cryptosporidium. The flu-like infection caused diarrhea, abdominal pains and vomiting. It got into the water supply from fecal matter at an upstream dairy farm.

A recent federal report says the water you drink may have been recycled from sewage waste back to drinking water five times!

In a Montreal study, families who did not filter their own water suffered 51% more colds, flu and digestive problems than did those who drank filtered water.

Lead, Radon, Mercury, Flouride, Pesticides

A great many other harmful substances may be in your drinking water. Last May, the EPA found unacceptable lead levels in over 800 municipal water systems.

The problem with lead is that it may come from the pipes in your own home or office, not from the municipal water system. The older the building, the greater the risk, since lead-containing solder used to be used on the joints of plumbing pipes.

They found unacceptable lead levels in the water at the U.S. Capitol, built in the 19th century. Maybe that's why our senators and congressmen sometimes seem mentally impaired.

If you've read a newspaper in the last twenty years, you also know that pesticides are found almost everywhere. The ground water in two California counties was found to be heavily contaminated with DBCP. This pesticide was banned in 1977 but it has a half-life of 141 years. That means half of it will still be around in the year 2118!

Play It Safe

I'm not trying to get you unduly alarmed here. The number of water-related cancer cases is fairly small. So is the number of infections. But the point is, why expose yourself at all?

If you decide on bottled water, make sure it's distilled. Don't buy spring water or filtered water because it may still be contaminated with bacteria, chlorine or other elements. The longer spring water sits on the shelf, the more bacteria it is likely to have.

In the long run you'll save money if you clean your water at home. It's also more convenient than hauling gallon jugs from the store. There are many water purification systems on the market.

Amway and Sears both market acceptable carbon filtering systems. Carbon filters are not perfect, but they are better than nothing. Carbon will remove chlorine and pesticides and some (but not all) heavy metals like lead. Unfortunately, carbon filters are not effective against bacteria and can even provide a home for them.

This isn't too much of a problem. *Most* city water systems will kill *most* bacteria with chlorine. What you then want to do is get the chlorine out. If you're still worried or if you are filtering well water, not city water, then boil your water for five minutes after you've filtered it. You can store the water in plastic containers as long as you let it cool off first.

The "gold standard" for purifying your water is a system that *distills your water and filters it*. These are more expensive, but you have the comfort of knowing there is no chlorine, fluoride, bacteria, viruses, pesticides or lead. You get nothing but H_2O. I know of at least six distiller systems on the market, including the WATERWISE 7000 (P.O. Box 4954, Center Hill, FL 33514). (I have no connection with this company and I don't profit if you decide to purchase.)

You'll be on your way to feeling younger if you take some of these suggestions. But next I'd like to help you *look* younger. . .

Chapter Thirteen

How to Keep Your Skin Soft and Youthful

If your skin is starting to dry out and crack like the rubber on an old windshield wiper, it's because free radicals have damaged both.

Skin gets wrinkled, old bread gets hard, plastic lawn furniture dries out and cracks, a rubber garden hose gets brittle and springs a leak. . .all for the same reason: They become "cross-linked" after bombardment by free radicals.

Ten years ago, students of aging probably would have told you that dry, wrinkled skin was programmed into your genes — part of the "aging process." Now we know better.

"Cross linking" is a key reason for aging and disease. You're going to hear a lot about it in years to come. But you don't have to wait to do something about it. Vitamins A, B-1, B-5, B-6, C, E, beta carotene, zinc and selenium can all slow down the cross-linking process.

Besides making your skin stiff and inflexible, cross linking affects all the organs in your body and makes them less able to do their jobs. Cross-linked arteries are hard. They lose their ability to pulse normally when your heart pumps blood. They can even blow out, resulting in internal bleeding.

The older we get, the stiffer we get, largely thanks to cross linking. Babies are so flexible they can suck their toes, but a female gymnast may end her career by age 20 because she progressively loses flexibility. An important protein called collagen provides the main support for all kinds of connective tissue, muscles, and blood vessels. As we age, our collagen becomes like a stiff windshield wiper or an old garden hose.

Some of the big offenders are X-rays, smoking, pollution, too much sun, and drinking. When you drink, your liver converts the alcohol into a potent cross-linker called acetaldehyde. This chemical is also found in cigarette smoke.

The person who smokes, drinks regularly, and spends a lot of time in the sun is a prime candidate for having skin like tanned leather — literally. The tanned leather in your shoes is animal skin that has been cross-linked to make it tougher.

One scientist has actually been able to remove the suntan from skin by repairing cross-link damage at the molecular level.

Your body does much the same thing on its own. It is constantly replacing and repairing damaged cells. It knows how to fight free radicals. But with the way we live and abuse ourselves, our bodies are bombarded with more free radicals than we can handle. By taking antioxidants, we help our bodies keep up with the damage. We can even get ahead of the game and reverse the damage.

According to biochemists Durk Pearson and Sandy Shaw, "You do have natural repair mechanisms which slowly replace cross-link damaged molecules. By using anti-cross-link nutrients, you can slow your rate of cross-link damage and give your overworked repair mechanisms a chance to catch up. This is a slow process, however, and requires plenty of patience. The time normally required to replace half the collagen in your body is several years. Don't expect to remove a half century of cross-linked tissue in a few months."

Pearson and Shaw give this fascinating example: Suppose free radicals are damaging one of your vital life support systems at the rate of ten percent per year. Your body can repair only nine percent, so you are losing ground at the rate of one percent annually. (It just so happens that we do age about one percent per year.)

Now suppose antioxidants can enable your body to keep up and repair all ten percent of the damage. The aging in that particular system will stop. If you go further — take antioxidants, correct a few bad habits — you can repair eleven percent and actually *gain ground* at the rate of one percent per year.

> Five years from today, you could have softer, more supple skin than you have now. That wouldn't be so bad, would it?

More important, you'll have softer, more supple arteries and muscles. And that could be the difference between life and death. You can fight off cancer, too, as the next chapter demonstrates. . .

Chapter Fourteen

Your Body Can Fight Off Cancer

One researcher bluntly says we know now what causes cancer: "Free radicals attack the DNA. Cancer results," says Professor Hari Sharma, MD, of the Ohio State University College of Medicine.

There's accumulating evidence that cancer occurs when free radicals damage the DNA in a cell. DNA is the cell's "management team." It is a very long molecule that contains all the information needed to make another you.

If you've seen the movie *Jurassic Park*, you know that in theory we could create a living dinosaur if we had a complete strand of its DNA.

Ordinarily this long strand is sprawled out in the middle of a cell like a ball of yarn after a kitten has played with it. It's an ideal target for a free radical to "nick" (the geneticist's term for injure).

A Berkeley scientist estimates that every cell in your body is attacked by free radicals 10,000 times a day. Each one of them would like to take a bite out of your DNA. With odds like that, it's a wonder we don't all have cancer.

Fortunately, your body has an amazing ability to repair itself. Remember, the last chapter mentioned this repair capacity. DNA happens to be extremely efficient — it can repair almost 100% of the damage it suffers. But it's the "almost" that can kill you — especially if you're not helping out with antioxidants.

Cancer doesn't occur every time a free radical nicks the DNA in one cell. Most such damage is either repaired or is not major in the first place. Cancer only follows when your DNA is damaged in a particular way. When that happens, the cancer cell stops being a liver cell or breast cell or whatever. It goes its own way, and starts reproducing in a runaway, out-of-control fashion.

Studies Link Free Radicals To Cancer

A Finnish study of 12,000 people found those with the lowest levels of antioxidants in their blood — vitamins A, E, and selenium — were eleven times more likely to get cancer.

In America, researchers have found that

cancer rates are lower in areas where there's a lot of selenium in the soil. On the other hand, low levels of selenium in the soil correlate with high cancer rates.

In Russia, scientists fed animals carcinogens and were able to detect high levels of free radicals in the liver. The levels increased for four months, then cancer began.

Even when free radical damage occurs, and the DNA fails to repair itself, you have another line of defense: your immune system. The cells in your immune system treat the cancer cells as invaders and literally eat them up. It's probable that we all fight off cancer this way every day.

> If you'd like to live to 120, the smartest thing you can do is pamper your immune system every way you can.

The immune system is a wonder that could keep you alive for 800 years if you could maintain it at youthful levels. If your doctor scraped a few of your skin cells or mouth cells and magnified them, he'd see deadly bacteria and viruses lurking among harmless ones. We all have these microorganisms inside and outside our bodies.

But we aren't all dead.

Fact number one: Most of us have healthy enough immune systems to fight off most diseases most of the time.

Fact number two: Most of us degrade our immune systems over time. Eventually, we *do* succumb to cancer, arthritis or other diseases that we *could* prevent with a healthy immune system. Partly due to AIDS, researchers are finally paying more attention to the immune system.

Those who suffer from AIDS tend to be in the forefront when it comes to an unhealthy lifestyle. They set themselves up with drug use, poor diet, lack of sleep, smoking, repeated venereal disease infections followed by repeated megadoses of antibiotics — all of which weaken the immune system. When they do encounter the AIDS virus they have no resistance. They roll over like tenpins.

The blood test for AIDS indicates whether a person has antibodies to the AIDS virus. *The blood test doesn't detect the AIDS virus itself — it detects the antibodies that your immune system produces to fight the virus.*

So a positive test means the person has been *exposed* to AIDS. *It can also mean he or she has successfully fought it off.* Doctors used to think that a positive HIV test was a death sentence. Now they know people can walk around for a decade or more with a positive blood test but no sign of the disease.

Don't get me wrong. These people are at risk. If their health gets run down they may get the disease. But right now, their immune systems are working.

There are people who have lived with AIDS victims for years without getting the disease. Instead of looking for a "miracle drug" to cure AIDS, we ought to study the immune systems of these people who *don't* get AIDS.

There are also many examples of "spontaneous remission" of cancer tumors — tumors that disappeared for no apparent reason, sometimes without treatment. The medical establishment pays little attention to this phenomenon. Yet it may hold the clue to a cancer cure.

Strengthen Your Immune System

Scientists have been able to take aging rats and improve their immune systems back to youthful levels. You can do much the same thing with your own immune system using food supplements.

- Selenium has been found to act as an anti-carcinogen. It prevents DNA damage.

- Vitamin A has been shown to stimulate the immune system and prevent the thymus — an important immune system gland — from growing smaller as you get older.

- A zinc deficiency can cause your thymus to shrink severely. Studies indicate most humans do not get enough zinc.

- Vitamin E is known to stimulate the immune system. Studies I've discussed in previous chapters link vitamin E to lower cancer risk.

Unfortunately, one of the ways the immune system kills invaders is by producing its *own* free radicals. And this process can get totally out of control.

What happens is your immune system makes a mistake and identifies some of your own cells as the enemy. There's evidence that this is what happens with multiple sclerosis and arthritis.

This new evidence gives us hope of tackling these diseases, as I'll show you in the next chapter. . .

Chapter Fifteen

New Hope for Arthritis Sufferers

The official position of the medical profession is that "the cause of arthritis is unknown." Most doctors will tell you it's "incurable" and you'll have to learn to live with it.

It used to be the official position that "There is no special diet for arthritis. No specific food has anything to do with causing it." That's what the Arthritis Foundation said in 1970.

Now, they've let it be known they're looking into "the question of how diet affects the immune system." But, they say, "It's too early to recommend any special diet."

While the medical profession tries to make up its mind, let's take a look at what arthritis is and what you can do about it.

If you've read this far, you won't be surprised: The cutting edge research shows free radicals play a prominent role. And — no

surprise again — the drugs and surgery rec-
ommended by the medical profession don't
work and *make the problem worse.*

The Cause of Arthritis

Arthritis literally means "inflammation
of the joint." That's all. It happens all the
time, to all of us. It has become a catch-all
term to describe almost any ache or pain.

If you strain yourself playing softball or
lifting a heavy bag, you may have "inflammation of the joint," but we certainly don't say
it's incurable. In fact, your body repairs such
injuries quite well. With age, however, many
of us fail to keep up with the damage and
develop pain in our joints.

This type of "wear and tear" is called
osteoarthritis. It's precisely what most people
have when they say they have arthritis. The
joints that carry the most weight — hips,
knees, and lower back — are where pain is
most common, although many people suffer
from hand and arm pain. The disease has
been observed in skeletons 40,000 years old,
and even in dinosaur skeletons!

What turns a temporary injury into a
chronic problem? The problem is that our
joints are covered with *cartilage* that is easy
to injure and not all that easy to repair. In the
worst case, you can wear all the cartilage
away from the joint so that bone is rubbing on

bone. That hurts!

Your joints also have that important connective tissue, collagen, to absorb shock and hold things together. We've already seen that free radicals damage collagen.

Cartilage poses a special problem because it receives no blood supply. It has its own fluid called synovial fluid. It requires your own bodily movements to squeeze waste out of cartilage and allow it to take in nutrients.

So basically your leg joint cartilage bears all your weight and doesn't have its own blood supply. Small wonder this is one of the first bodily systems to give out!

It is very significant that arthritis is an *inflammatory* disease. It's a medical fact that when a part of the body is inflamed your immune system bombards it with free radicals. This toxic shower of free radicals is one of the ways your body kills off invading microbes like flu. Your immune system produces its own free radicals all the time, by the trillions.

In the case of an injured joint, this body response is inappropriate and actually adds to the mayhem. A chain reaction — an *auto-immune* response — can set in as your body ends up fighting itself. The result is serious damage to the joints. The free radical attack breaks down your synovial fluid and membranes, cartilage and collagen.

Dr. Sharma says, "[T]he inflammatory response has an unfortunate tendency to feed on itself. Like an atomic reactor accelerating out of control, the first inflammatory interactions beget later ones in a cycle that is hard to break. If the inflammation lasts too long, the collateral damage becomes too great."

The extreme form of this autoimmune response is called *rheumatoid arthritis*. It affects fewer people — about seven million — but it attacks the whole body at once and it's much more serious than osteoarthritis.

Rheumatoid arthritis can be found among young people, often following a severe infection. Many individuals have solved their problem by tracing it to allergies or toxins. A thirty-five-year-old woman came down with system-wide joint pain after moving into a new house. It was so severe she needed crutches.

After getting away from the "sick building" she recovered. She also found out she had corn and cane sugar allergies. Like arthritis, allergies are another autoimmune disease, but I'm going to save that one for a future issue of my newsletter, *Healthy Longevity*. For now, I'll just repeat: Our diets and our environment are full of free-radical-producing toxins.

The first step is to recognize what the medical profession so far refuses to recognize: *Arthritis occurs when your immune system makes a mistake and attacks your body's normal tissues.* If you've read this book up to this point, you know one of the things you can do is load up on *antioxidants* to neutralize the attack.

There are two other important points about arthritis. . .

(1) It's very important to stop the process early. Permanent damage can occur, and it's almost impossible to repair.

(2) Mild exercise is extremely important because your own motions squeeze out waste and permit the cartilage to take in nutrients. *Every day, move every joint in your body in every direction it's made to go in.*

When you agree to try my newsletter for just one year, I'll send you a free copy of my special report, the **I Hate to Exercise Manual**. As the name implies, it's for the large majority of folks out there who just can't` get around to exercising. It outlines very simple easy exercises that take only minutes and can do you a world of good.

(If you're already a jock, don't worry: My newsletter has plenty of info for you, too. I'm a sports medicine doctor and a triathlete. So please turn to page 121 and place your order now!)

Pain-Killers Will Cause You More Pain

As with heart disease, stroke and cancer, conventional doctors do not have a clue as to what causes arthritis. Their only solutions are drugs and surgery. True to form, these treatments will make your arthritis worse.

The only program the medical system offers is pain relief. While that may not sound like a bad idea, pain-killers only *mask* pain. They treat the symptoms without getting to the cause, meanwhile making things worse with a battery of side effects.

• It's common to find arthritis patients taking two dozen aspirin a day. Unless you're really out of touch, you already know that aspirin causes bleeding of the stomach and may give you an ulcer. Maybe you don't know that aspirin depresses the immune system and sets you up for more illnesses.

• Other medications are nonsteroidal

anti-inflammatory drugs (NSAIDs). These include ibuprofen, which you may know under the brand names Motrin, Advil or Nuprin. One study says that NSAIDs kill 2,600 rhematoid arthritics per year and require 20,000 to be hospitalized. The drugs can cause gastrointestinal bleeding; worse yet, you won't even know it most of the time. The FDA attributes 10,000 to 20,000 deaths per year to NSAIDs.

- Even doctors admit a third type of drug is dangerous. These are the cortisone-like drugs called corticosteroids. Arthritis sufferers often beg for a "cortisone shot" because the relief can seem like a miracle. But it doesn't last long. When the pain returns it's even worse. Side effects include high blood pressure, diabetes, cataracts, bone loss (osteoporosis), ulcers, and immune system problems.

My program for arthritis has a good chance of stopping the deterioration of your joints if it's already started, and — more important — preventing damage if you're currently pain free. Besides a balanced program of food supplements, I'd like to see you start exercising. Work out within your limits so you don't injure yourself, gradually increasing your personal program.

I also want to see you avoid all the usual free radical culprits: stress, alcohol, smoking, a high-fat diet and tap water. But please, I don't expect miracles. I'd rather see you do one thing and stick to it.

If you feel better after a few months of antioxidants, write and tell me. I'd like to know! I want you to be happy. As the next chapter shows, it's more important than any of the other things I've discussed.

You Can't Separate Health and Happiness

If you've ever seen the musical *Guys and Dolls* you may remember Adelaide, who sings that "a person can develop a cold" just from waiting around year after year for her boyfriend to marry her.

Audiences have chuckled for decades at Adelaide's sniffles and sneezes because we all recognize the truth: We are more likely to get sick when we are unhappy or rundown.

It may console Adelaide to know that even if you have "that plain little band of gold" you can develop a cold. Researchers at Ohio State recently found that an argument with your spouse can depress your immune system — and a lot more than you think.

The same team has found that the immune systems of medical students go haywire during exam week. A similar effect is seen in older people who have taken care of a spouse with Alzheimer's over a long period of time.

FACT: Happiness strengthens your immune system.

FACT: Stress, depression and unhappiness weaken your immune system and set you up for disease.

FACT: Stress generates a flash flood of free radicals. Researchers have known for years that stress causes disease. There's now good reason to think it does so by creating those microscopic predators that we keep meeting in this book again and again. Hormones released by stress may also reduce your immunity.

When we're confronted with a traffic jam or a crisis at work, our bodies respond in the same way our ancestors responded to a sabertooth tiger attack. Our adrenal glands start pumping, our pulse and heart rates speed up, our energy soars. The body gets ready to fight or run away — the approriate way to handle a tiger but not very useful at the office or in a traffic back-up.

Your body prepares you to meet a crisis by raising your energy level. Whenever we burn food for energy, free radicals are a byproduct, but a healthy body can neutralize them with antioxidants. If you are constantly under pressure, though, the free radical overload can wear you out.

Exciting Discoveries
Are On the Way

The facts I've cited are just the tip of the iceberg. We're learning more and more about how our emotions affect our health. The exciting breakthroughs of the next 50 years are going to be in this area.

- A recent study showed that more heart attacks occur at 9 AM on Monday morning than any other time. Gee, I wonder why.

- In a 1991 study in the New England Journal of Medicine, 394 subjects were given nose drops that contained a cold virus. It turned out the amount of stress they were feeling at the time of exposure was directly related to whether they came down with a cold.

- A German study of 2000 subjects for 13 years found that individuals who suppress their emotions and fail to cope with stress were prime targets for cancer and heart disease. They experienced feelings of anger, depression, hostility and despair.

- A study in Finland involved over

13,000 men and women. There it was found that people with close ties to friends and family had less risk of death from all types of diseases.

• A similar study in Sweden followed 17,433 men and women for six years. The subjects ranged in age from 29 to 79. When adjusted for age, the figures show that those with the least amount of interaction with other people *were almost four times more likely to die* than those with the highest level of social interaction.

In the Swedish study, the lack of connection with other human beings had a stronger correlation with death rates than did smoking, exercise, job status, educational level or even the presence of chronic disease.

Conventional medicine is aware of these exciting discoveries, but it has no way of taking them in and using them to make you healthy. Their worldview just can't handle what's going on. It requires a whole new way of looking at things, and most doctors aren't ready for that yet. So the discoveries keep piling up.

You don't have to wait to put this knowledge to work for you. There's a whole battery of relaxation techniques you can use to neutralize the pressures of modern life. There's much more than I can cover here, but I talk about the subject every month in *Healthy Longevity*.

Laughter is one of the most effective ways to interrupt the stress that builds up in you during the day. I keep little wind-up toys on my desk that make me laugh. It's very hard to experience worry, fear or anger if you are laughing at a good joke or a funny movie, or if you're enjoying a happy tune.

Of course there's more to it if you really want to tackle stress. But if you are willing to take first one step, and then another, eventually they'll lead you to a very nice place: *a place where you really do feel good all the time*. You can control your own health.

What Michael Crichton Found Before the Dinosaurs

You may not know it, but Michael Crichton was trained as a doctor at Harvard Medical School before he decided to be a novelist. He recounts some of his experiences in his autobiographical book, *Travels*.

While working for a spell in a cardiology ward, he tried something unusual. He asked each patient, "Why did you have a heart attack?" Here's what he found:

"I feared they might respond with anger. So I started with the most easygoing patient on the ward, a man in his forties who had had a mild attack.

"Why did you have a heart attack?

"You really want to know?

"Yes, I do.

"I got a promotion. The company wants me to move to Cincinnati. But my wife doesn't want to go. She has all her family here in Boston, and she doesn't want to go with me. That's why."

According to Crichton, the man stated this calmly, with no anger. Other patients had similar answers:

"My wife is talking about leaving me. . ."

"My son won't go to law school."

"I didn't get the raise."

"I want to get a divorce and I feel guilty."

"My wife wants another baby and I don't think we can afford it."

Every patient had an answer, and not one of them mentioned hardening of the arteries, smoking, obesity, or the other standard risk factors.

Crichton writes, "These patients were telling me stories of events that had affected their hearts in a metaphysical sense. They were telling me love stories. Sad love stories, which had pained their hearts. Their wives and families and bosses didn't care for them. Their hearts were attacked. And pretty soon, their hearts were *literally* attacked."

The Fun Way to Lower Your Cholesterol

In an old study conducted in the 1970s, researchers at Ohio State University wanted to find out the effect that a high-cholesterol diet would have on rabbits. They expected the diet to damage the rabbits' health, and it did — in every group of rabbits except one.

In this one group, there were 60% fewer symptoms of disease. The researchers couldn't figure it out, until they discovered quite by accident that the student who fed these rabbits liked to pet them. Before feeding each rabbit, he would caress it for a few minutes. Amazing as it seems, that was enough to give the rabbits immunity to a toxic diet.

I don't know about you, but I'd rather lower my cholesterol by cuddling than by taking drugs! Sales of these drugs are approaching $2 billion a year. They don't work. The side effects include liver damage, constipation, headache, diarrhea and gas. These drugs also appear to have mind-altering qualities. Studies link them to depression, violence and suicide.

Every international study confirms there's a higher death rate among middle-aged men who take cholesterol-lowering drugs than among the control groups of men who don't. The higher overall death rates are due to higher rates of *violent* death, including suicide, probably linked to the mood-altering side effects.

Medicine: Still "Proving" that Babies Need to be Held

Looking at the beginning of life instead of the middle and the end, the medical profession has figured out that babies need cuddling. They die without it. This has been known for nearly 80 years.

You see, there used to be a great many abandoned babies in "foundling hospitals." And nearly all of them died. The death rate was almost 100%. One New York foundling hospital used to mark a baby's condition as hopeless on every admission card.

The medical profession finally figured out that the babies were dying because no one held them. They were never touched.

Recent studies have shown that when premature babies are frequently stroked —

even when in the incubator — they gain weight faster and have fewer complications than premature babies who are not stroked.

Foods You Eat Can Make You Happy or Sad, Well or Ill

Researchers have now linked depression to a lack of certain brain chemicals. Not only do we have lower levels of these chemicals when we're sad, but our immune systems also suffer. A person really *can* develop a cold.

Another thing we know is that levels of these chemicals tend to fall with age, and that's one of the reasons depression and illness are more likely.

The good news is you can boost your mood and your immune system with harmless substances available in food or in supplements.

One of the main causes of depression is the feeling that we're helpless, that events are beyond our control. When we're fighting a hopeless battle, we literally burn up a brain chemical called norepinephrine (NE). In a vicious cycle, the loss of this chemical even further reduces our ability to fight back. We sink further into depression.

In one experiment, researchers forced wild rats to swim until they became exhausted. The rats were able to last 60 hours. But if the investigator first held the rats tightly in his hands until they stopped struggling, then placed them in the water, they floundered and could only last about 30 minutes.

If you are helpless, depressed and without hope, you are more likely to fall victim to disease and so-called "old age." I'm sure you've noticed that elderly people in good health often die shortly after going into a nursing home or after losing a spouse.

You can learn to guide these feelings so that you stay well and happy. You can stimulate your brain's levels of NE and other "happiness hormones" through diet, food supplements, and relaxation techniques — and just getting a little sunlight during the winter!

I'd like to tell you about these, and much more, when you agree to try my monthly newsletter, *Healthy Longevity*.

If you do, you can get a free bonus report on a subject that interests nearly everyone, as you'll see. . .

Chapter Seventeen

Give Your Sex Life a Boost

You can boost your sex life at any age, even into your 90s. There's no reason to accept a declining sex drive as the natural outcome of the aging process.

In fact, one of the reasons people lose interest in sex is this foolish belief in the aging process. They think they're supposed to. And, by golly, they do! The first thing to do is change that belief.

Sure, some hormone levels go down with age. But there are certain ways these can be increased. I tell you how in a free bonus report called **Good Sex at Any Age**. There are even vitamins you can take a half hour or so before sex that may enhance your pleasure.

In this free booklet, you'll learn that genetic "aging clocks" in our bodies shut down hormone production, but there's some evidence these clocks aren't as "automatic" as we used to think. Disease, including free radical damage, can send a signal to your biological clocks that it's time to shut down.

When you take antioxidants, you reduce

this damage and your aging clocks don't run
so fast. Anything that reduces overall free
radical damage will probably boost your sex
drive as well.

There's even evidence that weight lifting
"fools" your body into thinking it's growing
again, provoking your glands to release tes-
tosterone, the male hormone that increases
sex drive and promotes muscle growth as
well.

For women, the free booklet talks about
the pros and cons of hormone replacement
therapy. With all due modesty, I think this
no-holds-barred, shoot-from-the-hip discus-
sion is the best thing I've seen on the subject.

What can you do now if you aren't enjoying sex as much or as frequently as you used
to? There are two things you should look at
right off:

(1) Are you or your spouse on medica-
    tions of any kind? Male impotence is a
    common side effect of tranquilizers
    and blood pressure drugs. But any
    other kind of drug is also suspect if
    your sex life has changed for the worse.

(2) Anything that damages your overall
    health and spirits is likely to damage
    your sex life. Diabetes is one of the
    most common causes of male impo-
    tence. It's a disease you can control by

cleaning up your diet. Depression and
stress are also common reasons people
lose interest in sex. Many people report an instant improvement as soon
as they shake depression.

You don't need to take mood-altering
drugs like Prozac and Valium to handle mild
depression or stress. Often, all you need to do
is stimulate your own body's production of
brain chemicals that have the same effect.

In Chapter Sixteen, I revealed that your
body uses up these brain chemicals, called
neurotransmitters, when you are in a hopeless situation. The lower your levels of neurotransmitters, the more hopeless you
feel.

Simple, safe food supplements can boost
your neurotransmitter levels and get you out
of this vicious cycle. There are also prescription drugs that have the same effect and are
much safer than tranquilizers. An estimated
25% of all cases of male impotence can be
corrected with a prescription drug I'll tell you
about in the free bonus report, **Good Sex at
Any Age**. Information on how to order may
be found on page 121.

If you are currently on medications I do
not recommend that you abruptly stop them.
Anything you do should be under your doctor's
supervision.

I've outlined a number of ways to control

your own diabetes and blood pressure, raise your energy level, and become happier and less stressed-out. Every method I've discussed is harmless and natural. If you subscribe to my newsletter, you'll be getting a lot more information.

There's no reason you can't gradually introduce these methods into your life while you gradually phase out drugs. And there's no reason your doctor should be unwilling to help you craft such a program.

In this book, I've provided the bare outlines of a program that will make you happy, healthy and full of energy. Every month in my newsletter, *Healthy Longevity* I flesh out my program with news and advice. I give you specific, proven techniques you can use.

It all depends on what shape you're in, but by the end of a year or two, I hope you are using my full program — diet, supplements, exercise and relaxation techniques. If you do, there's no doubt in my mind that you will feel great. By then, you will have forgotten that sexual performance or anything else was ever a problem for you.

You will feel good all the time. In the next chapter, there are more ways you can benefit. . .

Chapter Eighteen

Take Control of Your Health

I've enjoyed having this little visit with you. You see, I used to think I was a big, important surgeon and I didn't have much time to get to know people. It might have been just as well, since many of them didn't have long to live.

Now I'm a family doctor. I haven't wielded a scalpel since 1981. I have lots of time to get to know my patients, and they're living longer. Since quitting surgery, I've had the pleasure of seeing people get well. It's been a wonderful change in my life.

I don't have beepers or an answering service. My patients have my home number if they need to reach me. At the office, I answer the phone myself if my assistant happens to be out to lunch or gone for the day.

If you'd like to see what the medicine of the future will be like, come to my office. There's no one in the waiting room because I don't keep people waiting. My staff and I don't wear medical "costumes" — just street clothes. And I *listen* to people — sometimes for hours — because that's the best way to learn what makes you tick...and to find out why maybe you're not ticking properly at the moment.

It's probably not practical for you to come to my office, but the next best thing is to subscribe to my newsletter, *Healthy Longevity*. That way I can visit you every month.

In the pages of *Healthy Longevity* you'll receive much more detail than I can give you here about how to reverse or slow down the aging process, prevent high blood pressure, heart disease, cancer and arthritis, raise your energy level, and improve your sex life.

You'll learn more about items this book barely touched on: headaches, diabetes and allergies, for example.

My newsletter will also tell you a lot more about healthy eating habits. It would be too much to hit you with all at once. It's better to get one installment every month.

I also know that eating habits are hard to change, so you'll receive a lot of guidance on how to do it easily and with no effort.

My whole strategy is to help you gently favor good habits, not fight and struggle against bad habits. There's a way, for example, to cut down on smoking...not by going cold turkey in a nerve-wracking, life and death struggle. . .but simply by changing when and where you smoke.

Receive These Three Bonus Reports Just For Giving My Program a Try

I hope you are primed and ready to get started. If you are still a bit skeptical, I hope you'll extend me the courtesy of learning a little more about my program before making a final decision. I *know* it will work for you. But I want *you* to know it, totally. You can find out at absolutely no risk.

To help you get started, I will send you three free bonus reports when you subscribe:

FREE BONUS #1: The Most Important Medical Discovery of the Last 50 Years. This report gives you the vital details of the new free radical theory of disease and aging — the most important new medical theory since Louis Pasteur. You will learn how the ravenous molecular sharks called free radicals cause heart disease, atherosclerosis, cancer, and arthritis, and very likely allergies and multiple sclerosis as well. You can even use the remarkable discoveries to boost your energy level, stop skin wrinkling and improve your sex life. You will learn which antioxidants — *i.e.* vitamins and minerals — to take, when to take them, and how much, along with reliable, high-quality mail order sources.

FREE BONUS #2: Diet is a Four Letter Word. This report links heart disease, diabetes, cancer, and other diseases to a high-fat, high-sugar, low-fiber diet. But it's not my aim to lecture you about hard-to-break habits. In fact, this report will explain why crash diets never work and all the weight comes back, plus a few pounds. You'll learn the "secret" to successful dieting (which is actually not to diet at all). . .and a simple, gentle way to taper onto healthy eating habits so you barely notice your meals are changing. Each minor change you make will reward you richly with a higher energy level, a calmer stomach, fewer infections — and lower weight.

FREE BONUS #3: The I Hate to Exercise Manual. As the name implies, this special report is for people who are too busy or too tired to exercise — or just too glued to the couch to move. I propose a basic program that is incredibly simple and will take you only five minutes every morning. Yet you will notice benefits within weeks! Once you're started, I outline slightly more rigorous exercise ideas, including my favorite — a half hour walk several nights a week (proven to lower blood pressure and reduce your weight as much as a pound or two per month, besides combatting stress). I also give you more demanding exercise ideas — but you decide if and when you're ready.

Add it all up, and these three bonus reports give you an essential program that will gradually, easily change your life — and add to it as many as 20 years. The three reports are yours, free, when you subscribe for one year to my monthly newsletter, *Healthy Longevity*.

Subscribe for Two Years And Receive These Additional Free Reports

When you agree to try *Healthy Longevity* for two years, you get a discount from the one-year rate plus two more free bonus reports:

TWO-YEAR BONUS #1: **21st Century Medicine: Healthy at 100**— This report provides more detail for the "advanced" student who wants to know more about the relation between happiness and health. You'll see the amazing results you can achieve when you adopt the full program. Because when you get to the bottom of things, what makes you happy makes you healthy, and what makes you healthy makes you happy. That's why it's *easy* to taper onto the food, exercise and relaxation techniques I advocate. Unless you like being unhappy. (And believe it or not, there are people who do.)

TWO-YEAR BONUS #2: **Good Sex at Any Age**. This report explains how you can enjoy sex well into your 90s. It examines the common reasons sexual activity declines, and what you can do about it with food supplements, diet and exercise, and (in rare cases) prescription drugs. Just getting healthy — and getting off tranquilizers and blood pressure medications — is usually enough.

Good Sex at Any Age and **21st Century Medicine: Healthy at 100** are both yours when you subscribe for two years. You also receive the three bonus reports for one-year subscribers.

There are two additional benefits to being a subscriber. Both are more important than the bonus reports:

(1) Every month you will learn of the latest developments. New discoveries are being made all the time in the field of free radicals and antioxidants. I'm learning something new every day. It's a very exciting time in the health field and it's very important to stay tuned in. I'm applying the new re-

search in my practice, and I can tell you about real-life, actual benefits my patients are reaping. I'm also learning more every day about exercise techniques for both sexes and all age groups. There's a lot of news.

(2) As a monthly subscriber you'll be inspired and encouraged every month to stick with your new habits. Your life is probably busy and you may not think each and every day about the benefits of avoiding heart disease, cancer or arthritis 10 or 20 years down the road. My newsletter is a monthly pep talk to prove to you that you *can* feel good all the time and avoid the diseases of aging.

Money-back Guarantee

Finally, I want you to know that you are fully protected by my no-risk guarantee, whether you subscribe for one year or two years.

Read one, two or three issues of my newsletter. If you decide it's not for you, let me know and I'll send you a full refund, every penny you paid — no questions asked. Even after you've received four or more issues, I'll send you a refund for all remaining issues on your subscription. In either case the bonus reports and all issues you've received are yours to keep.

I'm not worried about sending a refund. I'm confident that if you change just one thing about your life, you'll feel better by the third issue. I have no doubt. And if you don't change one thing — if you don't at least take antioxidants — the newsletter would be a waste of your money.

There's a lot of exciting news in our editorial schedule for 1994. . .

- **Prostate problems:** The fate of every man over 50? I don't think so. Read about a natural way to cure harmless enlargement of the prostate. The pros and (mostly) the cons of surgery and radiation for prostate tumors. Why "watch and wait" may be the best strategy for prostate tumors.

- **The sport of the '90s.** Mild weight lifting has proven benefits for people of every age up to a hundred, as more people discover every day. Learn how to tailor a program to your age and physical condition.

- **The ultimate antioxidant:** A new

type of treatment under study by the FDA may be a drug-free "miracle cure" for hardening of the arteries. It's already used by about one thousand doctors to reverse athersclerosis and poisoning by lead, mercury and other toxins.

- **Frank talk about a taboo subject:** No, I don't mean sex, I mean constipation. People are so hung up about the subject that most of us aren't taught the basics. Millions of Americans think one or two bowel movements a week is "normal." Worse yet, thousands of doctors agree. The deadly consequences of poor elimination and what you can do about it.

- **Menopause doesn't exist in the Orient.** Is the "change of life" a lot of hooey? Find out in this upcoming article. (Also, Oriental males are more potent, guys. That's another upcoming article.)

- **Safe herbal remedies for a whole range of problems:** migraines, smoking, PMS, cavities, pimples, high cholesterol, corns. . .and much more! In many cases, expensive prescription drugs are inferior imitations of substances found in plants. (And by the way, if that sounds kooky to you, let

me tell you that many drugs like qui-
nine, aspirin and digitalis were origi-
nally "herbal remedies." The reason
our medical system doesn't research
herbal cures is there's no money in it.)

In addition to special features like these,
each and every issue of *Healthy Longevity*
carries regular departments on food supplements, exercise, diet, and ways to relax —
designed to reinforce your efforts in all four
areas.

You receive: three free bonus reports (five
reports for two-year subscribers). . .a complete money-back guarantee. . .and the chance
to live to be 120. I can't give you a better deal
than that. I hope you'll join me and thousands of other readers.

You really can feel good all the time.

Robert D. Willix, Jr., M.D.
August, 1994

*Special thanks to Lee Euler for his help in researching
and writing this book.*

No-Risk Introductory Subscription Offer

(For new subscribers only)

☐ **YES!** Rush all three FREE reports and enter my one-year (12 issue) introductory subscription to *Healthy Longevity* for $39 (regularly $64). (See reverse for more about FREE reports.) Plus, I may cancel anytime before my fourth issue and receive all my money back, or anytime thereafter for a prorated refund on remaining issues. In either case, the reports are mine to keep.

☐ **BEST DEAL:** I prefer a two-year subscription to *Healthy Longevity* for $75 because that way I can receive the special reports *21st Century Medicine: Healthy at 100* and *Good Sex at Any Age* in addition to the three reports for one-year subscribers.

☐ My payment for $39 ($75 for two years) is enclosed.
(Make checks payable to Healthy Longevity. MD residents add 5% sales tax.)

Daytime Phone Number: _____
(for order confirmation only)

☐ Charge my credit card: ☐ VISA
                ☐ MasterCard ☐ AMEX

Card #: _____

Expiration Date: _____

Signature: _____

Name _____

Address _____

City/State/Zip _____

Healthy Longevity • 824 E. Baltimore Street • PO Box 17477 • Baltimore, MD 21298 or fax (410) 539-7348

HB170

Sign up for a one-year, no-risk trial subscription to *Healthy Longevity*, at a $25 savings, and you'll receive your 3 FREE bonus reports:

The Most Important Medical Discovery of the Last 50 Years: The vital details of the new free radical theory of disease and aging, with the vitamin and mineral program you need to protect yourself. **Diet is a Four Letter Word:** Learn the secret to successful dieting (which is actually not to diet at

all). How to gradually learn eating habits that will help you lose weight and prevent the major diseases. **The I Hate to Exercise Manual:** For people who are too busy, tired, or unmotivated to exercise, a basic program that is incredibly simple and takes as little as five minutes a day.

FREE with 2-year subscription

21st Century Medicine: Healthy at 100: If you're serious about living long, read this probing report about the connection between happiness and health. You'll see the amazing results you can achieve when you adopt Dr. Willix's full program.

Good Sex at Any Age: The common reasons sexual activity declines, and what you can do about it with food supplements, diet and exercise and (in rare cases) prescription drugs.

100% Money-Back Guarantee

If you're not completely satisfied with *Healthy Longevity*, just let us know anytime before you receive your fourth issue and we'll refund the entire amount of your subscription. Promptly. With no questions asked. You don't have to send back the special reports. . .they're yours to keep, along with all issues you've received.

If you cancel after receiving four or more issues, we'll send you a prorated refund for all unmailed issues. . .and, again, you keep the bonus reports.

No-Risk Introductory Subscription Offer

(For new subscribers only)

☐ **YES!** Rush all three FREE reports and enter my one-year (12 issue) introductory subscription to *Healthy Longevity* for $39 (regularly $64). (See reverse for more about FREE reports.) Plus, I may cancel anytime before my fourth issue and receive all my money back, or anytime thereafter for a prorated refund on remaining issues. In either case, the reports are mine to keep.

☐ **BEST DEAL:** I prefer a two-year subscription to *Healthy Longevity* for $75 because that way I can receive the special reports *21st Century Medicine: Healthy at 100* and *Good Sex at Any Age* in addition to the three reports for one-year subscribers.

☐ My payment for $39 ($75 for two years) is enclosed.
(Make checks payable to Healthy Longevity. MD residents add 5% sales tax.)

☐ Charge my credit card: ☐ VISA ☐ MasterCard ☐ AMEX

Daytime Phone Number: _____
(for order confirmation only)

Card #: _____

Expiration Date: _____

Signature: _____

Name _____

Address _____

City/State/Zip _____

Healthy Longevity • 824 E. Baltimore Street • PO Box 17477 • Baltimore, MD 21298 or fax (410) 539-7348

HB171

Sign up for a one-year, no-risk trial subscription to *Healthy Longevity*, at a $25 savings, and you'll receive your 3 FREE bonus reports:

The Most Important Medical Discovery of the Last 50 Years: The vital details of the new free radical theory of disease and aging, with the vitamin and mineral program you need to protect yourself. **Diet is a Four Letter Word:** Learn the secret to successful dieting (which is actually not to diet at

all). How to gradually learn eating habits that will help you lose weight and prevent the major diseases. **The I Hate to Exercise Manual:** For people who are too busy, tired, or unmotivated to exercise, a basic program that is incredibly simple and takes as little as five minutes a day.

FREE with 2-year subscription

21st Century Medicine: Healthy at 100: If you're serious about living long, read this probing report about the connection between happiness and health. You'll see the amazing results you can achieve when you adopt Dr. Willix's full program.

Good Sex at Any Age: The common reasons sexual activity declines, and what you can do about it with food supplements, diet and exercise and (in rare cases) prescription drugs.

100% Money-Back Guarantee

If you're not completely satisfied with *Healthy Longevity*, just let us know anytime before you receive your fourth issue and we'll refund the entire amount of your subscription. Promptly. With no questions asked. You don't have to send back the special reports. . .they're yours to keep, along with all issues you've received.

If you cancel after receiving four or more issues, we'll send you a prorated refund for all unmailed issues. . .and, again, you keep the bonus reports.

 For faster service, FAX your special order to 410-539-7348

No-Risk Introductory Subscription Offer

(For new subscribers only)

☐ **YES!** Rush all three FREE reports and enter my one-year (12 issue) introductory subscription to *Healthy Longevity* for $39 (regularly $64). (See reverse for more about FREE reports.) Plus, I may cancel anytime before my fourth issue and receive all my money back, or anytime thereafter for a prorated refund on remaining issues. In either case, the reports are mine to keep.

☐ **BEST DEAL:** I prefer a two-year subscription to *Healthy Longevity* for $75 because that way I can receive the special reports *21st Century Medicine: Healthy at 100* and *Good Sex at Any Age* in addition to the three reports for one-year subscribers.

☐ My payment for $39 ($75 for two years) is enclosed.
(Make checks payable to Healthy Longevity. MD residents add 5% sales tax.)

Daytime Phone Number: _____
(for order confirmation only)

☐ Charge my credit card: ☐ VISA
 ☐ MasterCard ☐ AMEX

Card #: _____

Expiration Date: _____

Signature: _____

Name _____

Address _____

City/State/Zip _____

Healthy Longevity • 824 E. Baltimore Street • PO Box 17477 • Baltimore, MD 21298 or fax (410) 539-7348

HB172

Sign up for a one-year, no-risk trial subscription to *Healthy Longevity*, at a $25 savings, and you'll receive your 3 FREE bonus reports:

The Most Important Medical Discovery of the Last 50 Years: The vital details of the new free radical theory of disease and aging, with the vitamin and mineral program you need to protect yourself. **Diet is a Four Letter Word:** Learn the secret to successful dieting (which is actually not to diet at

all). How to gradually learn eating habits that will help you lose weight and prevent the major diseases. **The I Hate to Exercise Manual:** For people who are too busy, tired, or unmotivated to exercise, a basic program that is incredibly simple and takes as little as five minutes a day.

FREE with 2-year subscription

21st Century Medicine: Healthy at 100: If you're serious about living long, read this probing report about the connection between happiness and health. You'll see the amazing results you can achieve when you adopt Dr. Willix's full program.

Good Sex at Any Age: The common reasons sexual activity declines, and what you can do about it with food supplements, diet and exercise and (in rare cases) prescription drugs.

100% Money-Back Guarantee

If you're not completely satisfied with *Healthy Longevity*, just let us know anytime before you receive your fourth issue and we'll refund the entire amount of your subscription. Promptly. With no questions asked. You don't have to send back the special reports. . .they're yours to keep, along with all issues you've received.

If you cancel after receiving four or more issues, we'll send you a prorated refund for all unmailed issues. . .and, again, you keep the bonus reports.

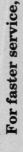 **For faster service, FAX your special order to 410-539-7348**

No-Risk Introductory Subscription Offer

(For new subscribers only)

☐ **YES!** Rush all three FREE reports and enter my one-year (12 issue) introductory subscription to *Healthy Longevity* for $39 (regularly $64). (See reverse for more about FREE reports.) Plus, I may cancel anytime before my fourth issue and receive all my money back, or anytime thereafter for a prorated refund on remaining issues. In either case, the reports are mine to keep.

☐ **BEST DEAL:** I prefer a two-year subscription to *Healthy Longevity* for $75 because that way I can receive the special reports *21st Century Medicine: Healthy at 100* and *Good Sex at Any Age* in addition to the three reports for one-year subscribers.

☐ My payment for $39 ($75 for two years) is enclosed.
(Make checks payable to Healthy Longevity. MD residents add 5% sales tax.)

Daytime Phone Number: _____
(for order confirmation only)

☐ Charge my credit card: ☐ VISA
☐ MasterCard ☐ AMEX

Card #: _____

Expiration Date: _____

Signature: _____

Name _____

Address _____

City/State/Zip _____

Healthy Longevity • 824 E. Baltimore Street • PO Box 17477 • Baltimore, MD 21298 or fax (410) 539-7348

HB173

Sign up for a one-year, no-risk trial subscription to *Healthy Longevity*, at a $25 savings, and you'll receive your 3 FREE bonus reports:

The Most Important Medical Discovery of the Last 50 Years: The vital details of the new free radical theory of disease and aging, with the vitamin and mineral program you need to protect yourself. **Diet is a Four Letter Word:** Learn the secret to successful dieting (which is actually not to diet at all). How to gradually learn eating habits that will help you lose weight and prevent the major diseases. **The I Hate to Exercise Manual:** For people who are too busy, tired, or unmotivated to exercise, a basic program that is incredibly simple and takes as little as five minutes a day.　　**HL894**

100% Money-Back Guarantee

FREE with 2-year subscription

21st Century Medicine: Healthy at 100: If you're serious about living long, read this probing report about the connection between happiness and health. You'll see the amazing results you can achieve when you adopt Dr. Willix's full program.

Good Sex at Any Age: The common reasons sexual activity declines, and what you can do about it with food supplements, diet and exercise and (in rare cases) prescription drugs.

☎　**For faster service, FAX your special order to 410-539-7348**　☎